AVERY LOCKE

Serverless architecture best practices for absolute Beginners

Contents

Introduction: Why Serverless Architecture?

T he rapid evolution of cloud computing has introduced a new paradigm in the way applications are built, deployed, and scaled. Serverless architecture has emerged as a revolutionary approach that offers greater flexibility, lower costs, and faster time-to-market, especially for developers and businesses looking to innovate. But what is serverless, and why has it become such a game-changer in modern application development?

In this book, **Serverless Architecture Best Practices for Absolute Beginners**, we'll dive deep into the foundational concepts, best practices, and practical applications of serverless architecture. Our goal is to make serverless accessible to everyone, whether you're a developer, an entrepreneur, or someone curious about how cloud computing is evolving.

By the end of this introduction, you'll understand what serverless architecture is, why it's gaining widespread adoption, and how you can use it to build scalable, efficient applications without worrying about infrastructure management. We'll also explore who this book is for and how you can best leverage the content to guide your learning journey.

What is Serverless?

At its core, serverless is a cloud computing execution model where the cloud provider dynamically manages the allocation and provisioning of servers. This means that developers no longer need to worry about the underlying infrastructure that runs their code or applications. Instead, they can focus purely on writing the logic that powers their applications while the cloud provider takes care of the scaling, maintenance, and management of servers.

However, the term "serverless" can be misleading. Despite its name, servers are still involved. The difference is that developers don't have to manage them directly. Cloud providers like AWS, Microsoft Azure, and Google Cloud handle the heavy lifting of provisioning, scaling, and maintaining the server infrastructure.

Serverless architecture is often associated with **Functions as a Service (FaaS)**, where small pieces of code, known as functions, are triggered by events and execute specific tasks. These functions run only when invoked, and you are billed only for the resources consumed during their execution. This is a significant departure from traditional server-based models where applications continuously run on dedicated servers, regardless of whether they are being used or not.

Beyond FaaS, serverless also encompasses **Backend as a Service (BaaS)**, where developers use managed services for backend components such as databases, authentication, file storage, and more. For example, AWS offers managed databases (Amazon DynamoDB), storage (Amazon S3), and APIs (Amazon API Gateway), allowing developers to build fully serverless applications by combining these services without maintaining the infrastructure behind them.

Key Characteristics of Serverless Architecture:

- **No Server Management**: Developers no longer need to provision, manage, or patch servers.
- **Automatic Scaling**: Serverless functions automatically scale in response to demand. Whether it's handling one request or millions, serverless

architecture can automatically adjust capacity.

- **Event-Driven Execution**: Serverless functions are often triggered by specific events, such as HTTP requests, file uploads, database changes, or messages from a queue.
- **Pay-Per-Use Pricing**: You only pay for the compute resources consumed during the execution of your functions, making it a cost-effective model for many use cases.
- **Short-Lived Stateless Functions**: Serverless functions are typically stateless, meaning they don't retain any data between invocations. Each function invocation is independent of the previous ones.

The Benefits of Going Serverless

Serverless architecture offers several advantages over traditional server-based models, making it an attractive option for developers and businesses alike. Let's explore the key benefits:

1. **Reduced Operational Overhead**

One of the most compelling benefits of serverless architecture is that it significantly reduces the operational burden on developers. In traditional server-based architectures, teams are responsible for provisioning, configuring, and maintaining servers, which involves tasks like patching, scaling, monitoring, and securing the infrastructure. Serverless abstracts away these responsibilities, allowing developers to focus purely on writing code and building features that directly impact the user experience.

This shift in responsibility from the development team to the cloud provider frees up valuable time and resources. Instead of spending hours managing infrastructure, developers can dedicate their efforts to innovation and creating better applications.

2. **Scalability**

Serverless architecture is inherently scalable. Cloud providers automatically handle the scaling of serverless applications in response to the number of incoming requests. This dynamic scaling allows applications to handle sudden spikes in traffic without requiring manual intervention.

For example, if you're running a traditional server-based application and experience a traffic surge, you might need to spin up additional servers or increase the capacity of existing ones. With serverless, this happens automatically. Whether your application is handling 10 requests per minute or 10,000, the cloud provider ensures that the necessary compute resources are available to meet demand.

3. Cost Efficiency

In traditional server-based architectures, you're typically charged for the uptime of your servers, regardless of whether they're actively being used. This leads to inefficient use of resources and higher operational costs. Serverless pricing models, on the other hand, are pay-per-use, meaning you only pay for the compute resources consumed during function execution.

This cost efficiency is particularly beneficial for applications with unpredictable or variable traffic patterns. For example, if your application experiences traffic spikes during specific periods (e.g., Black Friday sales, product launches), serverless can scale up to handle the load and scale down during periods of low demand, saving you money in the process.

4. Faster Time-to-Market

Serverless allows developers to build and deploy applications faster. By eliminating the need to manage infrastructure, developers can focus on writing and deploying code, leading to faster iteration cycles. Additionally, serverless platforms provide built-in integrations with various services, such as databases, APIs, and messaging systems, enabling developers to create feature-rich applications with minimal effort.

This agility is especially valuable for startups and businesses looking to bring products to market quickly. With serverless, development teams can rapidly prototype and launch applications, gathering user feedback and iterating on features without the delays typically associated with infrastructure management.

5. Improved Developer Productivity

With serverless, developers are no longer bogged down by managing servers, configuring networking, or dealing with scaling challenges. Instead, they can focus on what they do best: writing code. Serverless architecture encourages a modular, function-driven approach to development, where each function is responsible for a specific task or business logic.

This separation of concerns leads to more maintainable, testable, and reusable code. It also enables teams to work more efficiently, as different developers can focus on individual functions or services without stepping on each other's toes.

6. Environmental Impact

Serverless computing can also contribute to reducing an organization's carbon footprint. Traditional server-based models often involve over-provisioning resources to ensure high availability, leading to wasted energy and underutilized infrastructure. In contrast, serverless architecture optimizes resource allocation based on demand, leading to more efficient use of compute power.

By using only the resources needed at any given time, serverless reduces waste and helps minimize the environmental impact of running applications at scale.

Who Should Read This Book?

This book is designed for individuals who are new to serverless architecture and want to learn how to leverage its benefits to build scalable, cost-effective applications. It's ideal for:

- **Aspiring Developers and Software Engineers**: If you're new to the world of cloud computing and serverless, this book will guide you step-by-step through the core concepts and best practices, making complex topics approachable.
- **Entrepreneurs and Startups**: If you're looking to build and deploy applications quickly while keeping costs low, serverless is a great solution. This book will show you how to create applications that scale effortlessly, without the operational overhead.
- **Business Leaders and Project Managers**: For those involved in technology-driven businesses, understanding serverless architecture is

essential. This book will give you the knowledge to make informed decisions about cloud computing strategies and how serverless can benefit your organization.

- **IT Professionals and System Administrators**: While serverless reduces the need for traditional infrastructure management, understanding how it works is crucial for ensuring security, monitoring, and cost efficiency. This book will cover the key best practices you need to ensure smooth serverless operations.
- **Cloud Enthusiasts**: If you're curious about the future of cloud computing and want to learn how serverless is shaping the industry, this book will provide a thorough introduction and guide you toward mastery.

How to Use This Book

This book is structured to take you from the very basics of serverless architecture to more advanced topics like optimization, security, and scaling. You can either read it cover-to-cover or jump to sections that interest you the most. Here's a suggested way to use the book:

1. **Start with the Fundamentals**: If you're new to serverless, the first few chapters provide a solid foundation, explaining key concepts and helping you understand the advantages and trade-offs of serverless architecture.
2. **Follow Along with the Hands-On Examples**: Throughout the book, we provide practical examples and step-by-step tutorials that you can follow. We recommend trying these out in your own cloud environment (e.g., AWS, Azure, or Google Cloud) to gain hands-on experience.
3. **Apply the Best Practices**: The core of the book focuses on best practices for serverless architecture, covering performance, security, cost management, and more. These sections will help you design, build, and maintain robust serverless applications.
4. **Experiment and Build Projects**: As you progress through the book, try to build your own serverless projects based on the concepts you've learned. This will solidify your understanding and give you real-world

experience in serverless development.

5. **Use It as a Reference**: After completing the book, you can return to specific chapters as a reference when working on your own serverless projects. We've designed the book to be a practical guide that you can revisit whenever you need a refresher on key concepts or best practices.

Key Concepts You'll Learn

By the time you finish this book, you'll have a solid understanding of the following key concepts:

1. **What Serverless Architecture Is**: You'll learn the core principles of serverless computing and how it differs from traditional server-based models. You'll understand how functions are executed in response to events and how cloud providers handle infrastructure management.

2. **Serverless Platforms and Tools**: We'll cover popular serverless platforms like AWS Lambda, Azure Functions, and Google Cloud Functions. You'll also learn about tools like the Serverless Framework, AWS SAM, and other frameworks that simplify serverless development.

3. **Building and Deploying Serverless Applications**: You'll follow step-by-step tutorials to build your first serverless functions, integrate them with other cloud services, and deploy them in real-world scenarios.

4. **Best Practices for Serverless Architecture**: From performance optimization and cost management to security and scaling, you'll learn the best practices that will help you build efficient, reliable serverless applications.

5. **Advanced Serverless Topics**: We'll dive into advanced topics like event-driven architecture, microservices, and using serverless in AI, IoT, and machine learning workflows.

6. **The Future of Serverless**: You'll gain insights into the trends shaping the future of serverless computing and how it will impact the broader technology landscape.

Serverless architecture represents a new frontier in cloud computing, and understanding it is key to staying ahead in the ever-evolving tech industry. This book will equip you with the knowledge and tools you need to leverage the power of serverless architecture, enabling you to build scalable, cost-effective applications that are ready for the future. Let's dive in!

Chapter 1: The Evolution of Cloud Computing and Serverless

The journey of cloud computing has been marked by an ongoing push for greater efficiency, scalability, and simplicity in how businesses and developers build and manage applications. At the heart of this evolution is the growing popularity of serverless architecture, a model that offers unprecedented freedom from infrastructure management. To fully understand serverless, we first need to explore the broader context of cloud computing, from its early stages to the paradigm shift it represents today.

This chapter will take you through the evolution of cloud computing, the differences between traditional cloud models and serverless architecture, and how serverless fits into modern development. We'll also define key terms such as Functions as a Service (FaaS) and Backend as a Service (BaaS), both of which are central to the serverless computing model.

Traditional Cloud Models vs. Serverless

Cloud computing emerged as a solution to the limitations of on-premises infrastructure. Traditionally, organizations had to buy, configure, and maintain physical servers to run applications, which required significant upfront investment and technical expertise. Moreover, scaling applications required purchasing additional hardware, which often led to either underutilized or overburdened infrastructure. Cloud computing solved many of these problems by offering computing resources over the internet on a pay-as-you-go basis. Let's examine how traditional cloud models evolved and where serverless architecture fits into this story.

Traditional Cloud Models

The earliest form of cloud computing was **Infrastructure as a Service (IaaS)**, where cloud providers offered virtualized computing resources such as servers, storage, and networking. Companies like Amazon Web Services (AWS), Microsoft Azure, and Google Cloud provided scalable infrastructure that could be rented by businesses, eliminating the need for maintaining physical hardware.

With IaaS, businesses could create and manage their own virtual machines (VMs), which acted as servers in the cloud. These VMs could be scaled up or down based on demand, offering a level of flexibility that was impossible with physical servers. This model was a game-changer for businesses, as they no longer needed to worry about over-provisioning or under-provisioning hardware.

However, managing VMs still required significant operational overhead. IT teams had to configure operating systems, apply security patches, and monitor server health. This led to the rise of **Platform as a Service (PaaS)**, a more abstracted model where cloud providers offered complete platforms for developing, running, and managing applications. PaaS providers like Heroku and Google App Engine took care of the underlying infrastructure, allowing developers to focus on writing code.

Despite these advancements, both IaaS and PaaS required a certain level of infrastructure management. Developers still needed to think about provisioning resources, scaling, and maintaining server environments. This is where serverless architecture comes in, offering an even higher level of abstraction and efficiency.

Serverless: A Step Beyond PaaS

Serverless architecture represents a significant departure from traditional cloud models. In serverless, the cloud provider takes full responsibility for infrastructure management, including provisioning, scaling, and maintaining servers. Developers are only responsible for writing the code that runs in the cloud, and they are billed solely for the compute resources used during the execution of that code.

This is a radical shift from traditional models where developers or IT teams had to estimate and provision server capacity ahead of time. In serverless, there's no need to think about servers at all—hence the term "serverless." The cloud provider automatically scales the application based on demand, allowing businesses to handle unpredictable traffic spikes without having to over-provision resources.

Another key difference is the pricing model. In traditional cloud models, users are often charged based on server uptime, meaning they pay for the full duration that a server is running, regardless of whether it's being fully utilized. In serverless, you only pay for the actual execution time of your code, making it a much more cost-effective solution for applications with variable workloads.

Comparing Traditional Cloud Models and Serverless

AspectTraditional Cloud Models (IaaS/PaaS)Serverless Architecture

Server Management

Requires some degree of server management, including provisioning, patching, and scaling.

No server management required. The cloud provider handles everything.

Scalability

Scaling can be manual or automated, but requires provisioning resources.

Automatically scales based on demand.

Pricing

Pay for server uptime, regardless of utilization.

Pay only for the compute time used during function execution.

Deployment Complexity

Typically requires setting up environments and configuring servers.

Simplified deployment process. Focus on deploying code, not managing infrastructure.

Maintenance

Requires ongoing maintenance, such as applying patches and monitoring servers.

No maintenance required. The cloud provider handles updates and patches.

Use Cases

Ideal for applications requiring long-running processes and full control over infrastructure.

Ideal for event-driven applications, microservices, and applications with unpredictable traffic patterns.

How Serverless Fits Into Modern Development

In recent years, software development has seen a significant shift toward microservices, agile methodologies, and DevOps practices. These trends prioritize flexibility, speed, and the ability to iterate rapidly on features. Serverless architecture fits perfectly into this new way of developing applications, as it allows developers to build modular, scalable, and event-driven applications with minimal operational overhead.

Microservices and Serverless

Microservices architecture is an approach to building applications where different components, or "services," of the application are developed and deployed independently. Each microservice handles a specific business function, and they communicate with each other through APIs. This architecture offers numerous benefits, including improved scalability, easier maintenance, and faster development cycles.

Serverless complements microservices architecture by providing an easy way to deploy and manage these individual services. With serverless, each microservice can be deployed as a separate function, allowing it to scale independently based on demand. This makes it easier to build highly scalable applications without having to worry about over-provisioning resources for each microservice.

For example, consider an e-commerce application where different microservices handle user authentication, product search, and order processing. In a serverless architecture, each of these microservices can be deployed as independent functions. When traffic spikes during a flash sale, the cloud provider automatically scales each function to handle the load, ensuring that the application remains responsive without any manual intervention.

Event-Driven Architecture

Serverless is particularly well-suited for event-driven applications, where functions are triggered by specific events such as user actions, database changes, or messages from external systems. In this architecture, functions are invoked only when they are needed, making serverless a highly efficient model for applications with intermittent or unpredictable workloads.

For example, imagine an application that processes images uploaded by users. In a serverless architecture, a function could be triggered every time a new image is uploaded to a cloud storage service like Amazon S3. The function would automatically process the image—such as resizing or applying filters—and store the result in a database. This event-driven approach ensures that compute resources are only used when necessary, reducing costs and improving efficiency.

Agility and DevOps

In modern development, agility is key. Developers need to be able to iterate quickly, release new features, and respond to changes in user behavior without getting bogged down by infrastructure concerns. Serverless supports this agility by abstracting away infrastructure management and allowing developers to focus purely on writing code.

In a serverless environment, deployment is faster and simpler. Developers can push code directly to the cloud without worrying about setting up servers, configuring environments, or managing scaling policies. This streamlined deployment process enables more frequent releases and faster time-to-market for new features.

Moreover, serverless architecture aligns well with **DevOps** practices, which emphasize collaboration between development and operations teams. In a traditional environment, DevOps teams are responsible for managing the infrastructure and ensuring that applications run smoothly in production. With serverless, many of these operational tasks are automated by the cloud provider, allowing DevOps teams to focus on higher-level concerns such as monitoring, security, and optimization.

Key Terms: Functions as a Service (FaaS) and Backend as a Service (BaaS)

Now that we've explored the evolution of cloud computing and the role of serverless architecture in modern development, it's time to dive into two key concepts that define serverless: **Functions as a Service (FaaS)** and **Backend as a Service (BaaS)**.

Functions as a Service (FaaS)

FaaS is the core of serverless computing. It allows developers to write and deploy individual functions that are executed in response to specific events. These functions are stateless, meaning they don't retain any data between executions. Each function is invoked independently and is only executed when triggered by an event.

With FaaS, developers can build applications as a collection of functions, each responsible for a specific task or piece of business logic. These functions can be triggered by a variety of events, such as HTTP requests, database updates, or messages from an external system.

How FaaS Works

1. **Write the Function**: Developers write a small piece of code (the function) that performs a specific task. This function could be anything from processing an image to querying a database.
2. **Define the Trigger**: The function is triggered by an event, such as an HTTP request, a file upload, or a message in a queue. The event serves as the input for the function.
3. **Execute the Function**: When the event occurs, the cloud provider automatically provisions the necessary resources to execute the function. The function runs, processes the event, and returns a result.
4. **Billing**: You are charged only for the execution time of the function, making FaaS a cost-effective model for event-driven applications.

Example Use Cases for FaaS

- **API Backends**: FaaS is commonly used to build serverless APIs, where each function represents an individual API endpoint. For example, an e-commerce website might have separate functions for handling user login, product search, and order processing.
- **Data Processing**: FaaS is ideal for processing large volumes of data in real-time. For example, a function could be triggered every time a new log entry is added to a database, allowing the function to analyze the log data and store insights in a separate system.
- **Automation**: FaaS can be used to automate repetitive tasks, such as resizing images, sending notifications, or performing routine maintenance tasks in cloud environments.

Backend as a Service (BaaS)

While FaaS focuses on the execution of functions, BaaS refers to the use of managed services for common backend components such as databases, authentication, storage, and messaging. BaaS providers offer ready-to-use services that developers can integrate into their applications without having to build and maintain backend infrastructure themselves.

With BaaS, developers can leverage services provided by cloud platforms like AWS, Azure, and Firebase to handle backend operations, allowing them to focus on building frontend features and application logic. For example, instead of managing a database server, developers can use a managed database service like DynamoDB or Firebase Firestore.

Common BaaS Services

- **Authentication**: Managed authentication services like AWS Cognito and Firebase Authentication allow developers to implement user authentication and authorization without building their own systems.
- **Databases**: Managed database services like Amazon DynamoDB, Azure Cosmos DB, and Firebase Firestore provide scalable, fully-managed databases that can be easily integrated into serverless applications.
- **File Storage**: Services like Amazon S3 and Firebase Storage allow developers to store and retrieve files without having to manage the

underlying storage infrastructure.

- **Messaging**: Managed messaging services like Amazon SNS, Azure Service Bus, and Firebase Cloud Messaging provide reliable, scalable messaging capabilities for serverless applications.

Example Use Cases for BaaS

- **Mobile Applications**: BaaS is widely used in mobile app development, where developers can leverage services like Firebase to handle user authentication, data storage, and push notifications without needing to build a custom backend.
- **Web Applications**: For web applications, BaaS services like AWS Amplify provide everything from authentication to APIs, making it easier to build feature-rich applications without managing the backend infrastructure.
- **IoT Applications**: BaaS can simplify the development of IoT applications by providing managed services for device communication, data storage, and real-time event processing.

Conclusion

In this chapter, we've explored the evolution of cloud computing and the rise of serverless architecture as a powerful tool for modern application development. Serverless represents a significant departure from traditional cloud models, offering developers the freedom to focus on building features without worrying about infrastructure management. By leveraging **Functions as a Service (FaaS)** and **Backend as a Service (BaaS)**, developers can build scalable, event-driven applications that are cost-effective and easy to maintain.

Serverless architecture fits seamlessly into modern development practices such as microservices, event-driven architecture, and DevOps, making it an ideal solution for businesses looking to innovate quickly and efficiently. In the following chapters, we'll dive deeper into how you can get started with serverless architecture, explore best practices, and build real-world applications using the concepts we've introduced here.

Chapter 2: How Serverless Works

S erverless architecture is a significant shift in how applications are built, deployed, and maintained. It simplifies development by removing the need for developers to manage servers, while providing an efficient and scalable way to run applications. But to truly understand how serverless works, it's important to dive into its core mechanics: event-driven architecture, serverless execution models, and the processes that happen behind the scenes. In this chapter, we'll explore how serverless operates and what makes it an ideal choice for modern applications.

Event-Driven Architecture

At the heart of serverless computing is **event-driven architecture**. This design paradigm emphasizes that system components—such as services, microservices, and functions—react to specific events. These events can originate from user actions (such as a mouse click), changes in data, messages from other services, or external systems interacting with your application.

Understanding Event-Driven Architecture

In an event-driven system, events are the key elements that trigger the system's response. An event can be anything, such as a user making an HTTP request, a file being uploaded, or a message arriving in a queue. These events serve as inputs that initiate specific business logic, encapsulated within functions or services, that process the event and generate the desired output.

Here's how a basic event-driven workflow works in a serverless environment:

1. **Event Source**: An event source generates an event. This could be a wide range of triggers, including:

- HTTP requests (via API Gateway)
- File uploads (via services like AWS S3)
- Database updates (via DynamoDB streams or triggers)
- Time-based events (via cloud provider cron jobs like AWS CloudWatch Events)
- Message queues (via AWS SQS, Azure Queue Storage, etc.)

1. **Event Listener**: The event listener detects the event generated by the event source and invokes a corresponding function. In serverless environments, this listener is often managed by the cloud provider itself, automatically detecting events and triggering the appropriate function.
2. **Event Processor (Function)**: The triggered function processes the event and performs the necessary task, such as writing to a database, sending a notification, or returning data to the user. In serverless, this is commonly a **Function as a Service (FaaS)**, such as an AWS Lambda function, Azure Function, or Google Cloud Function.
3. **Outcome**: After processing the event, the function may return a response, trigger another event, or interact with other services. The function runs only for the duration necessary to handle the event and then terminates, ensuring efficient resource usage.

This architecture contrasts with traditional monolithic applications, which are typically designed to run continuously, regardless of whether or not they are handling requests.

Benefits of Event-Driven Architecture

1. **Scalability**: Because functions are triggered on demand, event-driven

systems can scale automatically in response to the number of incoming events. There's no need to manually scale resources, as cloud providers handle scaling based on the number of events to process.

2. **Decoupling**: Event-driven systems promote decoupling between components, meaning that each function or service can operate independently. This makes the system more resilient to failures and easier to maintain. For example, if one service experiences an issue, it doesn't impact other services that aren't directly connected to it.

3. **Efficiency**: Functions are executed only when an event occurs, reducing idle time and lowering costs. You only pay for the compute time when your function is actively running, which is particularly useful for workloads with unpredictable traffic patterns.

4. **Modularity**: In an event-driven system, each function performs a discrete task. This modularity improves code maintainability, testability, and flexibility, as you can modify or update individual functions without impacting the overall system.

Common Event Sources in Serverless Systems

Cloud providers offer a variety of event sources that can trigger functions in a serverless environment. Some common examples include:

- **HTTP API Requests**: Users can send HTTP requests via API Gateways, which can trigger serverless functions. For example, AWS API Gateway is commonly used to trigger Lambda functions in response to user requests.
- **File Uploads**: Uploading a file to a storage service like Amazon S3 or Google Cloud Storage can generate an event that triggers a function to process the file, such as generating thumbnails or analyzing the content.
- **Database Changes**: Some cloud providers offer event-driven database triggers. For instance, DynamoDB streams can trigger Lambda functions whenever there is a change to the database, such as an insert or update.
- **Message Queues**: Services like AWS SQS (Simple Queue Service) or Azure Queue Storage can send messages that trigger functions to process tasks asynchronously. This is useful for workloads that require reliable,

decoupled message passing between services.

- **Scheduled Events**: Time-based events can be set to trigger serverless functions at regular intervals using services like AWS CloudWatch Events or Azure Timer Triggers. This is useful for running periodic tasks like backups or batch processing.

Serverless Execution Models

Serverless execution models are the core mechanism by which serverless functions run in response to events. These models determine how the cloud provider handles function invocation, scaling, resource allocation, and billing.

There are two primary types of execution models in serverless computing: synchronous and asynchronous. Each has different use cases and characteristics based on how functions are invoked and how they return results.

Synchronous Execution

In a synchronous execution model, the client (or event source) waits for the function to complete its task and return a response. This model is commonly used for real-time applications, where immediate feedback is necessary, such as APIs or web applications.

How Synchronous Execution Works

1. **Event Trigger**: An event, such as an HTTP request or a user action, triggers the function.
2. **Function Invocation**: The cloud provider provisions the resources needed to execute the function, which is then invoked.
3. **Execution and Response**: The function performs its task, such as querying a database, performing calculations, or generating a response to the client. Once the task is complete, the function returns a response to the client.
4. **Billing**: The client is charged based on the duration of the function execution.

Example Use Cases for Synchronous Execution

- **APIs**: Synchronous execution is ideal for building APIs, where a client (such as a web or mobile app) sends a request and expects an immediate response. For example, when a user submits a form on a website, an API Gateway might trigger a serverless function to process the input and return a result.
- **Real-Time Applications**: Any application requiring real-time feedback, such as chat applications or live dashboards, benefits from synchronous execution.

Asynchronous Execution

In an asynchronous execution model, the client does not wait for the function to complete its task. Instead, the function is triggered, and the client continues its work without needing an immediate response. Asynchronous functions are typically used for background tasks, batch processing, or tasks that take a long time to complete.

How Asynchronous Execution Works

1. **Event Trigger**: An event, such as an email notification or a message arriving in a queue, triggers the function.
2. **Function Invocation**: The cloud provider provisions the necessary resources and invokes the function asynchronously, meaning the client does not wait for a response.
3. **Execution**: The function performs its task independently of the client. Once the task is complete, the function can trigger other events or services if necessary.
4. **Billing**: The client is charged for the compute resources consumed during function execution, but since it's asynchronous, the client isn't involved in waiting for completion.

Example Use Cases for Asynchronous Execution

- **Background Processing**: Asynchronous execution is ideal for processing tasks that can run in the background, such as sending emails, processing images, or handling large datasets.

- **Message Queues**: In systems using message queues (such as AWS SQS or Azure Queue Storage), functions can be triggered to process messages without requiring immediate feedback to the user.
- **Batch Jobs**: Asynchronous execution works well for running batch jobs that process large amounts of data over time, such as generating reports or processing log files.

Cold Starts in Serverless Execution Models

One of the unique characteristics of serverless execution models is the concept of **cold starts**. A cold start occurs when a serverless function is invoked for the first time after a period of inactivity. When this happens, the cloud provider needs to provision the necessary resources (such as containers or VMs) to run the function, which can introduce a slight delay in execution.

Cold starts can affect both synchronous and asynchronous execution, but they are more noticeable in synchronous workflows, where users are expecting immediate feedback. The delay introduced by a cold start typically lasts a few hundred milliseconds but can vary depending on the cloud provider and the size of the function.

To mitigate the impact of cold starts, developers can:

- **Keep functions warm** by periodically invoking them to prevent the cloud provider from deallocating resources.
- **Use smaller function packages** to reduce the time it takes for the cloud provider to initialize the function.
- **Optimize function code** to reduce dependencies and lower initialization time.

What Happens Behind the Scenes?

Serverless computing abstracts much of the infrastructure management away from developers, but understanding what happens behind the scenes can provide insight into the benefits and limitations of this model. While developers interact with serverless services at a high level, cloud providers handle many complex tasks under the hood to ensure that functions run smoothly.

Provisioning and Execution

When a function is triggered in a serverless environment, the cloud provider is responsible for provisioning the resources needed to execute the function. This process typically involves
several steps:

1. **Trigger Detection**: The cloud provider continuously monitors for incoming events that can trigger functions. When an event occurs, the provider detects it and identifies the corresponding function to invoke.
2. **Resource Allocation**: The cloud provider allocates the necessary resources (such as containers or VMs) to run the function. This involves provisioning compute capacity, setting up networking, and loading the function code.
3. **Function Initialization**: The cloud provider initializes the function, which may include loading dependencies, setting up execution environments, and initializing any required context.
4. **Function Execution**: The cloud provider invokes the function and executes the code in response to the event. During this phase, the function performs its logic, processes input data, and generates output.
5. **Resource Cleanup**: After the function execution is complete, the cloud provider may deallocate the resources used to run the function, especially if it has not been invoked for a while. This is part of the pay-as-you-go model, where users are only charged for the resources consumed during function execution.

Monitoring and Logging

Monitoring and logging are critical components of serverless architecture, as they provide visibility into the performance and behavior of functions. Cloud providers offer integrated monitoring tools that allow developers to track metrics, set up alerts, and analyze logs.

- **Metrics**: Metrics provide insights into function performance, including invocation counts, execution duration, error rates, and cold start occurrences. Developers can use these metrics to identify performance bottlenecks, optimize function code, and improve the overall efficiency of their applications.
- **Logs**: Logging captures detailed information about function execution, including input data, output data, and any errors encountered during processing. Logs are invaluable for debugging and troubleshooting issues, as they provide a detailed account of what happened during function execution.

Security Considerations

Security is an important consideration in serverless architecture. While cloud providers handle much of the infrastructure security, developers must still consider several aspects to ensure their applications remain secure:

1. **Permissions and Access Control**: Developers need to carefully manage permissions for serverless functions to prevent unauthorized access to sensitive data or resources. This often involves configuring IAM (Identity and Access Management) roles and policies to restrict access to specific services and resources.
2. **Data Handling**: When processing events, developers must ensure that sensitive data is handled securely. This includes encrypting data in transit and at rest, validating input data, and implementing secure coding practices.
3. **Isolation and Multi-Tenancy**: Serverless functions run in a multi-tenant environment, meaning that multiple functions from different users may share the same underlying infrastructure. Developers should be aware of potential security vulnerabilities and ensure that their functions are isolated from one another.

Conclusion

In this chapter, we explored the inner workings of serverless architecture, focusing on event-driven architecture, serverless execution models, and the processes that occur behind the scenes when functions are invoked. Event-driven architecture allows applications to respond dynamically to various events, promoting scalability and efficiency. We also examined the synchronous and asynchronous execution models, highlighting their respective use cases and how they operate within the serverless paradigm.

Understanding how serverless works provides valuable insight into the advantages it offers, such as reduced operational overhead, automatic scaling, and cost efficiency. As we continue our journey through serverless architecture in the following chapters, you will gain a deeper appreciation for how to effectively leverage this innovative approach to building applications.

Chapter 3: Common Serverless Platforms

S erverless computing has revolutionized how developers build and deploy applications. With cloud providers managing the infrastructure, developers are free to focus solely on writing code. This shift has given rise to several serverless platforms, each with unique features and benefits tailored to specific user needs.

In this chapter, we'll dive into the three most popular serverless platforms: **AWS Lambda, Azure Functions**, and **Google Cloud Functions**. We will explore their features, strengths, and weaknesses, and provide a detailed comparison to help you determine which platform might be the best fit for your serverless needs.

Overview of AWS Lambda, Azure Functions, and Google Cloud Functions

AWS Lambda

AWS Lambda is the pioneer of the serverless computing model, introduced by Amazon Web Services in 2014. Lambda quickly became a popular choice for developers because of its seamless integration with the entire AWS ecosystem, providing powerful event-driven execution and enabling the creation of serverless microservices, APIs, and automation tasks.

Key Features of AWS Lambda:

- **Event-Driven Execution**: AWS Lambda functions are triggered by various AWS services, such as Amazon S3 (file uploads), Amazon DynamoDB (database changes), and Amazon SNS (notifications), as well as external events like HTTP requests through Amazon API Gateway.
- **Granular Billing**: With AWS Lambda, you only pay for the execution time of your function. Billing is based on the number of function invocations and the duration of execution, measured in milliseconds.
- **Auto-Scaling**: Lambda automatically scales in response to the number of requests, eliminating the need to manually configure or provision infrastructure.
- **Extensive Language Support**: AWS Lambda supports multiple programming languages, including Node.js, Python, Java, Ruby, Go, and .NET Core.
- **Integration with AWS Ecosystem**: One of the major advantages of Lambda is its tight integration with the rest of the AWS services. You can easily connect Lambda functions with services like Amazon S3, DynamoDB, Kinesis, and CloudWatch, among others.
- **Security**: AWS Lambda offers strong security features, including built-in integration with AWS Identity and Access Management (IAM) for role-based access control, as well as VPC (Virtual Private Cloud) support to ensure network isolation.
- **Custom Runtimes**: In addition to the natively supported languages, AWS Lambda allows you to create custom runtimes, giving you the flexibility to run any language or framework that isn't directly supported by AWS.

Use Cases for AWS Lambda:

- **Data Processing**: Automatically processing files uploaded to S3 or streams from Kinesis and DynamoDB is a common Lambda use case.
- **Real-Time Web Applications**: Lambda can handle HTTP requests via API Gateway, making it suitable for building backends for web and mobile applications.

- **Automation**: AWS Lambda can be used to automate routine infrastructure tasks, such as scaling resources, backups, or triggering workflows when changes occur in the environment.
- **IoT Backends**: AWS Lambda can process messages from IoT devices using AWS IoT Core, making it a powerful option for IoT applications.

Azure Functions

Azure Functions is Microsoft's serverless computing platform, introduced in 2016. Azure Functions aims to provide a highly productive environment for building serverless applications, particularly within the Microsoft ecosystem. While it's often favored by developers already using Azure services, Azure Functions offers a flexible, language-agnostic environment and features that appeal to a broad audience.

Key Features of Azure Functions:

- **Event-Driven Programming Model**: Similar to AWS Lambda, Azure Functions is built around an event-driven model where functions are triggered by events such as HTTP requests, queue messages, or changes in Azure Storage.
- **Timer-Based Execution**: Azure Functions natively supports the execution of scheduled tasks using time-based triggers (via CRON expressions), which is useful for batch jobs and automated maintenance tasks.
- **Seamless Integration with Azure Services**: Azure Functions integrates tightly with services like Azure Blob Storage, Cosmos DB, Azure Event Hubs, and Azure Service Bus. This integration enables developers to easily connect their functions with data and messaging services within the Azure ecosystem.
- **Multiple Hosting Plans**: Azure Functions offers several hosting options, including:
- **Consumption Plan**: Similar to AWS Lambda's billing model, the consumption plan charges users based on the number of executions and execution time, with automatic scaling.
- **Premium Plan**: For scenarios requiring more predictable scaling

and performance, the premium plan provides dedicated resources and support for virtual network (VNet) connectivity.

- **Dedicated Plan**: Users can also run Azure Functions on dedicated VMs, providing complete control over performance and scaling.
- **Durable Functions**: Azure provides a framework for long-running serverless functions called **Durable Functions**. This allows developers to write stateful workflows using functions that can maintain state between executions, overcoming one of the common limitations of traditional serverless architectures.
- **Support for Various Programming Languages**: Azure Functions supports a range of programming languages, including C#, JavaScript, Python, Java, TypeScript, and PowerShell.

Use Cases for Azure Functions:

- **Scheduled Tasks**: With native support for time-based triggers, Azure Functions is great for executing tasks like backups, data cleanup, or sending periodic emails.
- **Event-Driven Automation**: Like AWS Lambda, Azure Functions excels at handling event-driven workflows, such as processing blobs in Azure Storage or responding to messages from Service Bus queues.
- **API Backends**: Azure Functions can act as lightweight API backends, handling HTTP requests from users and returning dynamic data.
- **Business Process Automation**: Using Durable Functions, developers can build complex workflows that involve multiple tasks, such as order processing or multi-step data pipelines, while maintaining state across executions.

Google Cloud Functions

Google Cloud Functions is Google's fully managed, event-driven serverless compute platform. Launched in 2018, Google Cloud Functions has quickly gained traction among developers, particularly those working within the Google Cloud ecosystem. It provides similar functionality to AWS Lambda and Azure Functions, but with a focus on Google's services like Firebase, BigQuery, and Google Cloud Storage.

Key Features of Google Cloud Functions:

- **Event-Driven Execution**: Google Cloud Functions is designed to be triggered by events from Google Cloud services, including Cloud Storage, Firestore, Pub/Sub, and HTTP requests. It enables a broad range of use cases, from handling API requests to automating data processing tasks.
- **Auto-Scaling**: Like AWS Lambda and Azure Functions, Google Cloud Functions automatically scales based on the number of incoming requests, ensuring that you only pay for what you use.
- **Tight Integration with Google Cloud Ecosystem**: Google Cloud Functions integrates seamlessly with Google's other services, making it an ideal choice for developers already using Google's cloud stack. For instance, it integrates with Firebase, a popular backend-as-a-service (BaaS) platform for mobile and web applications.
- **Simplified Deployment**: Google Cloud Functions focuses on simplicity, making it easy for developers to deploy functions directly from the command line or via the Google Cloud Console. This ease of use is a significant advantage for small teams or individuals looking to deploy applications quickly.
- **Real-Time Data Processing**: Google Cloud Functions can process real-time events from Google Cloud services like Pub/Sub, Firestore, and BigQuery, enabling the development of highly reactive systems.

Use Cases for Google Cloud Functions:

- **Real-Time Data Processing**: Google Cloud Functions is particularly well-suited for handling real-time events from Pub/Sub and Firestore, making it ideal for applications that require real-time data pipelines or stream processing.
- **Mobile App Backends**: When combined with Firebase, Google Cloud Functions can act as a backend for mobile and web applications, handling

tasks like authentication, database queries, and push notifications.

- **Automation**: Google Cloud Functions can automate tasks such as processing files in Cloud Storage or running scheduled jobs like data imports or batch processing.
- **Cloud-Native Applications**: Google Cloud Functions is a natural fit for cloud-native applications that leverage other Google Cloud services such as BigQuery, Cloud Datastore, and Cloud Firestore.

Comparing Platform Features

Now that we've examined AWS Lambda, Azure Functions, and Google Cloud Functions individually, let's compare their features head-to-head to help you understand which platform might be the best fit for your needs.

FeatureAWS LambdaAzure FunctionsGoogle Cloud Functions

Launch Year

2014

2016

2018

Languages Supported

Node.js, Python, Java, Go, Ruby, .NET

C#, JavaScript, Python, Java, PowerShell

Node.js, Python, Go, .NET, Java

Scaling

Automatic

Automatic with more control options

Automatic

Triggering Events

API Gateway, S3, DynamoDB, Kinesis, etc.

Blob Storage, Cosmos DB, Service Bus, HTTP

Pub/Sub, Firestore, Cloud Storage

Integrations

Tight integration with AWS services

Strong integration with Azure services

Tight integration with Google Cloud services, especially Firebase

Cold Start Delay

Moderate to low

Moderate to low

Low to moderate

Custom Runtimes

Supported

Limited support

Limited support

Durable Workflows

AWS Step Functions

Durable Functions

Workflows using Google Cloud Workflows

VPC Support

Full VPC integration

VNet integration in premium plans

VPC connector for private networking

Billing

Pay-per-request and execution time

Pay-per-request and execution time

Pay-per-request and execution time

Max Execution Time

15 minutes

Up to 230 minutes (Dedicated Plan)

9 minutes

Maximum Memory Allocation

10 GB

14 GB

16 GB

Deployment Complexity

Requires setup with API Gateway for HTTP

Simplified deployment with various triggers

Simplified deployment

Which Platform is Right for You?

Choosing the right serverless platform depends on several factors, including your technical requirements, the cloud services you're already using, and the overall complexity of your project. Below, we'll break down which platform might be the best fit based on various criteria:

1. Integration with Existing Cloud Services

- **AWS Lambda**: If your application is already hosted on AWS or heavily relies on AWS services such as S3, DynamoDB, Kinesis, or CloudWatch, then AWS Lambda is the best choice. Its deep integration with the AWS ecosystem ensures seamless connectivity and minimizes complexity when building end-to-end serverless applications.
- **Azure Functions**: If you're already using Azure services like Azure Storage, Cosmos DB, or Service Bus, Azure Functions provides the most seamless experience. Azure Functions is also ideal for enterprises heavily invested in the Microsoft stack, including .NET and Azure DevOps.
- **Google Cloud Functions**: If your application relies on Google Cloud services, especially Firebase, Google Cloud Functions is an excellent choice. It's particularly suited for developers building mobile or web applications with Firebase as the backend or working with Google's big data services like BigQuery and Pub/Sub.

2. Programming Language and Runtime Support

- **AWS Lambda**: AWS Lambda offers extensive support for popular programming languages, including Node.js, Python, Java, Go, Ruby, and .NET Core. Additionally, AWS Lambda supports custom runtimes, allowing you to bring your own runtime for any language not natively supported.
- **Azure Functions**: Azure Functions is a strong contender if you're working with C# or other .NET languages, as Microsoft's ecosystem is natively integrated. Azure Functions also supports a wide range of

other languages, including JavaScript, Java, Python, and PowerShell.

- **Google Cloud Functions**: Google Cloud Functions supports fewer languages compared to Lambda but covers the essentials: Node.js, Python, and Go. If you're working primarily with JavaScript or Python in a Google Cloud-native environment, this platform offers a straightforward and developer-friendly experience.

3. Performance and Latency (Cold Starts)

- **AWS Lambda**: AWS Lambda has made significant improvements in reducing cold start latency, especially when using Provisioned Concurrency, a feature that pre-warms functions to reduce startup time. This makes it a good choice for latency-sensitive applications that require low startup times.
- **Azure Functions**: Cold starts in Azure Functions are generally moderate, but users on the Premium Plan or with Durable Functions may experience reduced latency. Azure Functions also offers VNet integration for reduced latency when accessing private resources.
- **Google Cloud Functions**: Google Cloud Functions generally exhibits lower cold start times compared to AWS Lambda, particularly for smaller functions. It's a good choice for real-time applications or APIs where latency is a concern.

4. Long-Running Processes

- **AWS Lambda**: Lambda is limited to a maximum execution time of 15 minutes, which makes it unsuitable for long-running processes. However, for most use cases that require quick execution, Lambda performs well.
- **Azure Functions**: Azure Functions has a significant advantage in long-running processes, especially with its Dedicated Plan, which allows for functions to run for up to 230 minutes. The Durable Functions framework also makes it possible to implement long-running workflows with state management.

- **Google Cloud Functions**: Google Cloud Functions is limited to a maximum execution time of 9 minutes, making it less ideal for long-running tasks compared to Azure Functions. However, it's sufficient for short to moderate tasks, especially in real-time and event-driven applications.

5. Cost Efficiency

- **AWS Lambda**: AWS Lambda follows a pay-per-use pricing model, where users are charged based on the number of requests and the duration of function execution. It's highly cost-effective for workloads with unpredictable traffic, as you only pay for the compute time used.
- **Azure Functions**: The consumption plan of Azure Functions offers similar pricing to AWS Lambda, with automatic scaling and pay-per-execution costs. However, Azure's Dedicated Plan allows for more predictable costs when you need reserved resources for long-running or resource-heavy tasks.
- **Google Cloud Functions**: Google Cloud Functions also follows a pay-as-you-go model, charging based on the number of invocations and the duration of execution. It's cost-competitive for small to medium-sized workloads and excels in use cases where Firebase and Google Cloud services are heavily used.

6. Developer Ecosystem and Tools

- **AWS Lambda**: AWS offers an extensive set of developer tools, such as AWS Cloud9 for cloud-based development environments, AWS SAM (Serverless Application Model) for building and deploying serverless applications, and a rich ecosystem of services to complement Lambda.
- **Azure Functions**: Microsoft's Visual Studio and Visual Studio Code integration make developing and deploying Azure Functions seamless, especially for developers already familiar with the Microsoft stack. Azure DevOps also integrates well with Azure Functions for CI/CD pipelines.

- **Google Cloud Functions**: Google Cloud Functions emphasizes simplicity, with a streamlined deployment process and minimal setup. Google's tools like Firebase, Firestore, and BigQuery make it an attractive option for building cloud-native applications quickly. The Google Cloud SDK also provides robust CLI tools for managing functions.

Conclusion

Choosing the right serverless platform depends on your specific use case, existing cloud infrastructure, and preferred development environment. AWS Lambda, Azure Functions, and Google Cloud Functions each offer robust, scalable serverless solutions, but their strengths lie in different areas:

- **AWS Lambda** excels in integration with AWS services, offers extensive language support, and is ideal for developers already using the AWS ecosystem.
- **Azure Functions** provides a flexible, highly integrated solution for enterprises working with Azure services and the Microsoft stack, and it is particularly strong for long-running processes with its Durable Functions and Premium Plan.
- **Google Cloud Functions** is a natural choice for developers working within Google's ecosystem, especially for Firebase-backed mobile applications or real-time data processing using Google Cloud services.

Ultimately, the right platform for you will depend on your project's specific requirements, including integration with cloud services, performance needs, and cost considerations. As serverless computing continues to evolve, all three platforms are likely to introduce new features and improvements, making serverless an increasingly attractive option for developers building scalable, efficient applications.

Chapter 4: Getting Started with AWS Lambda

AWS Lambda has become one of the most popular serverless computing platforms, enabling developers to run code without provisioning or managing servers. In this chapter, we will guide you through the process of getting started with AWS Lambda. We'll cover how to set up your AWS account, create and deploy your first Lambda function, and build a hands-on example of a serverless API.

Setting Up Your AWS Account

Before diving into AWS Lambda, you need an AWS account. If you already have one, you can skip this section. If not, follow these steps to set up your account.

Step 1: Create an AWS Account

1. **Visit the AWS Website**: Go to the AWS homepage.
2. **Click on "Create a Free Account"**: Look for the button that says "Create a Free Account" and click on it. AWS offers a free tier, which allows you to explore many services without incurring costs.
3. **Enter Your Email Address**: Fill in your email address and choose a password. You will also need to provide an account name.

4. **Choose an Account Type**: Select "Personal" or "Professional" based on your needs. This choice primarily influences the initial setup.

5. **Provide Contact Information**: Fill out your contact information, including your full name, address, and phone number.

6. **Payment Information**: Enter your credit card information. AWS may require this for verification purposes, even if you plan to use free tier services.

7. **Identity Verification**: AWS will send a verification code to your phone number. Enter this code to continue.

8. **Select a Support Plan**: Choose a support plan. For most beginners, the "Basic Support" plan, which is free, is sufficient.

9. **Complete the Sign-Up**: Review your information and complete the signup process. AWS will send a confirmation email once your account is active.

Step 2: Access the AWS Management Console

1. **Log In**: Go to the AWS Management Console and log in using the email and password associated with your account.

2. **Navigate the Console**: The console is the main dashboard for managing your AWS services. From here, you can access all AWS services, including Lambda.

Building and Deploying Your First Lambda Function

Now that you have your AWS account set up, it's time to create your first AWS Lambda function. In this section, we will walk through the process step-by-step.

Step 1: Navigate to AWS Lambda

1. **Access the Services Menu**: In the AWS Management Console, click on the "Services" dropdown menu in the top left corner.

2. **Find Lambda**: In the "Compute" section, click on "Lambda." This will

take you to the AWS Lambda dashboard.

Step 2: Create a Lambda Function

1. **Click on "Create Function"**: On the Lambda dashboard, click on the "Create function" button.
2. **Select "Author from Scratch"**: You will see three options for creating a function. Select "Author from scratch."
3. **Configure the Function**:

- **Function Name**: Enter a name for your function (e.g., MyFirstLambdaFunction).
- **Runtime**: Choose the runtime for your function. For this example, select **Node.js 14.x** (or the latest version available).
- **Permissions**: Leave the default option "Create a new role with basic Lambda permissions" selected. This will create a new role that grants your function basic permissions to run.

1. **Click "Create Function"**: After filling in the details, click the "Create function" button. AWS Lambda will create your function and take you to the function configuration page.

Step 3: Write Your Function Code

1. **Code Editor**: You will see a code editor on the configuration page. AWS provides a built-in code editor where you can write your Lambda function code. You can also upload a ZIP file with your code or use Amazon S3 to store your code.
2. **Write Sample Code**: Replace the default code with the following simple function that returns a greeting:

```javascript
javascript
Copy code
exports.handler = async (event) => {
    const message = 'Hello from AWS Lambda!';
    return {
        statusCode: 200,
        body: JSON.stringify({ message }),
    };
};
```

1. **Save Changes**: Click the "Deploy" button in the upper right corner to save your changes.

Step 4: Test Your Lambda Function

1. **Configure a Test Event**: In the Lambda console, scroll down to the "Test" section. Click on "Configure test events."
2. **Create a Test Event**: Choose "Create new test event," give it a name (e.g., TestEvent), and keep the default event JSON. You can use the following JSON for a simple test:

```json
json
Copy code
{
    "key1": "value1"
}
```

1. **Save the Test Event**: Click the "Create" button to save your test event.
2. **Run the Test**: Now click on the "Test" button. This will invoke your Lambda function with the test event you just created.

Step 5: Review the Output

1. **Check the Results**: After the function runs, you will see the results in the console. The output should display the status code (200) and the greeting message:

```json
Copy code
{
    "statusCode": 200,
    "body": "{\"message\":\"Hello from AWS Lambda!\"}"
}
```

Congratulations! You have successfully created and tested your first AWS Lambda function.

Hands-On Example: Creating a Serverless API

In this section, we will build a simple serverless API using AWS Lambda and Amazon API Gateway. This API will provide a GET endpoint that returns a greeting message. Follow these steps to create your serverless API.

Step 1: Create a New Lambda Function for the API

1. **Return to the Lambda Dashboard**: Click on "Functions" in the left navigation panel to return to the Lambda dashboard.
2. **Create a New Function**: Click on the "Create function" button again.
3. **Configure the Function**:

- **Function Name**: Enter a name for your API function (e.g., GreetingAPI).
- **Runtime**: Choose **Node.js 14.x** (or the latest version available).
- **Permissions**: Leave the default option "Create a new role with basic Lambda permissions" selected.

1. **Click "Create Function"**: Click the "Create function" button to create your new Lambda function.

Step 2: Write the API Function Code

1. **Code Editor**: Once the function is created, replace the default code in the code editor with the following code to create a simple greeting API:

```javascript
Copy code
exports.handler = async (event) => {
    const message = 'Hello, welcome to the Serverless API!';
    return {
        statusCode: 200,
        body: JSON.stringify({ message }),
    };
};
```

1. **Save Changes**: Click the "Deploy" button in the upper right corner to save your changes.

Step 3: Create an API Gateway for the Lambda Function

1. **Navigate to API Gateway**: Go to the AWS Management Console, click on the "Services" dropdown, and select "API Gateway."
2. **Create a New API**: Click on the "Create API" button.
3. **Choose API Type**: Select "HTTP API" for this example, as it provides a simpler setup for RESTful APIs.
4. **Configure the API**:

- **API Name**: Enter a name for your API (e.g., GreetingAPI).
- **Description**: Optionally, provide a description for your API.
- **Endpoint Type**: Choose "Regional" to create an API that can be accessed from within a specific region.

1. **Click "Next"**: Click the "Next" button to continue.

Step 4: Integrate the API with Your Lambda Function

1. **Configure Routes**: In the API Gateway console, click on "Add Integration."
2. **Choose Lambda Function**: Select "Lambda function" as the integration type.
3. **Select Your Function**: In the Lambda function field, search for the function you created (e.g., GreetingAPI) and select it.
4. **Configure Method**: Set the method to **GET**, which allows users to retrieve data from your API.
5. **Click "Next"**: After configuring the integration, click the "Next" button.

Step 5: Deploy the API

1. **Create a Stage**: You'll be prompted to create a new deployment stage. Enter a stage name (e.g., dev) and click "Next."
2. **Review and Create**: Review your settings, and click "Create" to deploy your API.
3. **Access Your API URL**: After deploying, you will see an API endpoint URL. Copy this URL as you'll use it to test your API.

Step 6: Test Your Serverless API

1. **Open a Web Browser or API Testing Tool**: You can use a web browser or tools like Postman or curl to test your API.
2. **Make a GET Request**: Paste the API endpoint URL into the address bar (or use it in Postman) and make a GET request. You should receive a response similar to this:

```
json
Copy code
```

```
{
    "message": "Hello, welcome to the Serverless API!"
}
```

Congratulations! You have successfully created a simple serverless API using AWS Lambda and API Gateway. This API can now be called from web or mobile applications, enabling you to build powerful, scalable serverless applications.

Managing Your Lambda Function and API

Once you have your Lambda function and API set up, it's essential to understand how to manage and optimize them for production use.

Monitoring Your Lambda Function

AWS provides built-in monitoring and logging capabilities for Lambda functions through Amazon CloudWatch. Here are some key metrics to monitor:

1. **Invocation Count**: The number of times your function is invoked. This metric helps you understand the usage patterns of your function.
2. **Duration**: The average time taken to execute your function. Monitoring duration can help you identify performance issues and optimize your code.
3. **Error Rate**: The percentage of invocations that result in errors. Keeping track of errors is crucial for maintaining application reliability.
4. **Throttles**: The number of times your function is throttled due to exceeding the concurrent execution limit. This can help you identify capacity issues.

To access these metrics:

1. **Go to CloudWatch**: In the AWS Management Console, search for and select "CloudWatch."

2. **Navigate to Metrics**: Click on "Metrics" in the left navigation panel.
3. **Select Lambda Metrics**: Choose "Lambda" to view the metrics related to your Lambda functions.

Setting Up Logging

AWS Lambda automatically logs output from your functions to Cloud-Watch Logs. You can add logging statements to your code to capture additional information for debugging purposes.

For example, modify your API function to include logging:

```javascript
Copy code
exports.handler = async (event) => {
    console.log('Received event:', JSON.stringify(event, null, 2));
    const message = 'Hello, welcome to the Serverless API!';
    return {
        statusCode: 200,
        body: JSON.stringify({ message }),
    };
};
```

Now, whenever your function is invoked, you can view the logs in the CloudWatch Logs console.

1. **Access CloudWatch Logs**: In the CloudWatch console, click on "Logs" in the left navigation panel.
2. **Find Your Log Group**: Locate the log group for your Lambda function (named /aws/lambda/<function-name>).
3. **View Log Streams**: Click on the log group to see individual log streams for each invocation.

Optimizing Your Lambda Function

To get the most out of your AWS Lambda function, consider the following optimization strategies:

1. **Reduce Package Size**: Minimize the size of your deployment package by only including necessary libraries and dependencies. Use tools like webpack to bundle your code and remove unused files.
2. **Optimize Code Performance**: Identify bottlenecks in your code and optimize them for better performance. Consider using asynchronous programming models where applicable.
3. **Use Provisioned Concurrency**: For applications that require consistent low latency, consider using Provisioned Concurrency. This feature keeps a specified number of instances warm, reducing cold start times.
4. **Tune Memory Allocation**: AWS Lambda allows you to allocate memory ranging from 128 MB to 10 GB. Increasing memory not only affects the memory available for your function but also increases the CPU power allocated to it. Experiment with different memory settings to find the optimal configuration.

Conclusion

In this chapter, we have guided you through the process of getting started with AWS Lambda, from setting up your AWS account to building and deploying your first Lambda function. You've learned how to create a simple serverless API and test it, providing a foundation for building more complex serverless applications.

AWS Lambda offers a powerful platform for building event-driven, scalable applications without the need for server management. With its seamless integration with other AWS services, built-in monitoring and logging, and robust optimization features, Lambda is an excellent choice for developers looking to embrace the serverless model.

As you continue your journey into serverless computing, remember to explore AWS documentation, experiment with different use cases, and leverage the many features AWS Lambda has to offer. In the next chapters, we will delve deeper into advanced topics, best practices, and real-world applications of AWS Lambda to help you become proficient in serverless architecture.

Chapter 5: Introduction to Serverless Frameworks

As serverless computing continues to gain traction, various frameworks have emerged to simplify the development and deployment processes. These frameworks provide tools, templates, and abstractions that help developers create serverless applications efficiently. In this chapter, we will explore some of the most popular serverless frameworks, including Serverless Framework, AWS SAM (Serverless Application Model), and AWS Chalice. We will discuss their features, benefits, and how they can enhance your serverless development experience.

Understanding Serverless Frameworks

Serverless frameworks are designed to streamline the process of building, deploying, and managing serverless applications. They allow developers to focus on writing code rather than worrying about the underlying infrastructure. By using these frameworks, you can take advantage of best practices, templates, and built-in tools to enhance your serverless development process.

Why Use Serverless Frameworks?

1. **Simplified Development**: Frameworks provide a structured way to develop serverless applications, reducing the complexity associated with

managing cloud resources and configurations.

2. **Rapid Deployment**: Most frameworks come with tools that automate the deployment process, allowing you to deploy your applications with a single command.

3. **Built-in Best Practices**: Frameworks often incorporate best practices for serverless architecture, such as resource management, monitoring, and security, helping you avoid common pitfalls.

4. **Integration with CI/CD**: Many frameworks support continuous integration and deployment (CI/CD) pipelines, making it easier to automate your deployment processes.

5. **Multi-Cloud Support**: Some frameworks are designed to work across multiple cloud providers, enabling you to build and deploy applications in a cloud-agnostic manner.

1. Serverless Framework

The **Serverless Framework** is one of the most widely used frameworks for building serverless applications. It was created to simplify the deployment of serverless applications across various cloud providers, including AWS, Microsoft Azure, Google Cloud Platform, and more.

Key Features of Serverless Framework

- **Multi-Provider Support**: The Serverless Framework allows you to build applications that can run on different cloud providers, enabling flexibility in choosing your cloud environment.
- **YAML Configuration**: Configuration for your serverless application is defined in a single YAML file (serverless.yml), making it easy to manage resources, functions, events, and environment variables.
- **Plugins and Extensions**: The Serverless Framework has a rich ecosystem of plugins that extend its functionality. These plugins can help with deployment, monitoring, authentication, and other tasks.
- **Built-in Monitoring**: The framework provides built-in monitoring and debugging tools to help you troubleshoot and optimize your serverless

applications.

- **Easy Integration**: The Serverless Framework seamlessly integrates with various services, enabling you to connect your functions to APIs, databases, storage, and more.

Getting Started with the Serverless Framework

To get started with the Serverless Framework, follow these steps:

1. **Install Node.js**: The Serverless Framework requires Node.js. Download and install it from the Node.js website.
2. **Install Serverless Framework CLI**: Open a terminal and run the following command to install the Serverless Framework globally:

```bash
Copy code
npm install -g serverless
```

1. **Create a New Serverless Service**: Use the Serverless CLI to create a new service. Run the following command, replacing my-service with your desired service name:

```bash
Copy code
serverless create --template aws-nodejs --path my-service
```

1. **Navigate to Your Service Directory**:

```bash
bash
Copy code
cd my-service
```

1. **Configure Your Serverless.yml File**: Open the serverless.yml file in your favorite code editor. This file defines your service configuration, including functions, events, and resources. Here's a simple example:

```yaml
yaml
Copy code
service: my-service

provider:
  name: aws
  runtime: nodejs14.x

functions:
  hello:
    handler: handler.hello
    events:
      - http:
          path: hello
          method: get
```

1. **Write Your Function Code**: Open the handler.js file and implement your function logic. Here's a simple example:

```javascript
javascript
Copy code
'use strict';

module.exports.hello = async (event) => {
```

```
    return {
        statusCode: 200,
        body: JSON.stringify({
            message: 'Hello from Serverless Framework!',
        }),
    };
};
```

1. **Deploy Your Service**: Use the following command to deploy your service to AWS:

```bash
Copy code
serverless deploy
```

1. After deployment, you will receive an endpoint URL that you can use to access your function.

2. AWS SAM (Serverless Application Model)

AWS SAM is an open-source framework specifically designed for building serverless applications on AWS. SAM simplifies the process of defining, deploying, and managing serverless resources using a single YAML configuration file.

Key Features of AWS SAM

- **Native AWS Integration**: As an AWS-native framework, SAM provides deep integration with AWS services such as Lambda, API Gateway, DynamoDB, and more.
- **Simplified Configuration**: SAM uses a simplified syntax for defining serverless resources in a single template.yaml file. This makes it easier to

manage your application's infrastructure.

- **Local Development and Testing**: SAM CLI allows developers to test and debug their applications locally before deploying to the cloud. You can simulate AWS Lambda and API Gateway behavior on your local machine.
- **Built-in Best Practices**: SAM encourages best practices for serverless architecture, such as versioning, monitoring, and secure resource access.
- **Easy CI/CD Integration**: AWS SAM integrates well with AWS Code-Pipeline and other CI/CD tools, making it easier to automate your deployment workflows.

Getting Started with AWS SAM

To get started with AWS SAM, follow these steps:

1. **Install AWS CLI**: Make sure you have the AWS CLI installed and configured with your AWS account credentials. Follow the instructions on the AWS CLI installation page.
2. **Install AWS SAM CLI**: Download and install the AWS SAM CLI from the AWS SAM CLI installation page.
3. **Create a New SAM Application**: Use the following command to create a new SAM application:

```bash
Copy code
sam init
```

1. You will be prompted to select a template. Choose the one that fits your needs (e.g., "AWS Quick Start Templates").
2. **Navigate to Your Application Directory**:

```bash
bash
Copy code
cd my-sam-app
```

1. **Configure Your SAM Template**: Open the template.yaml file, which defines your serverless resources. Here's a simple example:

```yaml
yaml
Copy code
AWSTemplateFormatVersion: '2010-09-09'
Transform: AWS::Serverless-2016-10-31
Description: Simple SAM Application

Resources:
  HelloWorldFunction:
    Type: AWS::Serverless::Function
    Properties:
      Handler: app.hello
      Runtime: nodejs14.x
      Events:
        HelloApi:
          Type: Api
          Properties:
            Path: /hello
            Method: get
```

1. **Write Your Function Code**: Open the app.js file and implement your function logic. Here's an example:

```javascript
javascript
Copy code
'use strict';
```

```
exports.hello = async (event) => {
    return {
        statusCode: 200,
        body: JSON.stringify({
            message: 'Hello from AWS SAM!',
        }),
    };
};
```

1. **Build Your SAM Application**: Use the following command to build your application:

```bash
Copy code
sam build
```

1. **Deploy Your SAM Application**: Use the following command to deploy your application to AWS:

```bash
Copy code
sam deploy --guided
```

1. This command will guide you through the deployment process and create an AWS CloudFormation stack for your application.

3. AWS Chalice

AWS Chalice is a Python-based framework developed by AWS for building serverless applications. Chalice is designed to simplify the process of creating and deploying serverless APIs and applications using AWS Lambda and API Gateway.

Key Features of AWS Chalice

- **Python-Centric**: Chalice is built specifically for Python developers, making it an excellent choice for those familiar with the language. You can write your application using standard Python syntax and libraries.
- **Automatic API Gateway Integration**: Chalice automatically generates API Gateway configurations based on your code, enabling you to create APIs effortlessly.
- **Local Development Server**: Chalice provides a built-in local development server that allows you to test your application before deploying it to AWS.
- **Easy Deployment**: Deploying a Chalice application is straightforward, requiring only a single command to publish your application to AWS.
- **Integration with AWS Services**: Chalice makes it easy to integrate with various AWS services, such as DynamoDB, S3, and SNS.

Getting Started with AWS Chalice

To get started with AWS Chalice, follow these steps:

1. **Install AWS Chalice**: Ensure you have Python and pip installed. Then, install Chalice using the following command:

```bash
Copy code
pip install chalice
```

1. **Create a New Chalice Application**: Use the following command to create a new Chalice application:

```bash
Copy code
chalice new-project my-chalice-app
```

1. **Navigate to Your Application Directory**:

```bash
Copy code
cd my-chalice-app
```

1. **Edit Your Chalice Application**: Open the app.py file to define your application logic. Here's a simple example:

```python
Copy code
from chalice import Chalice

app = Chalice(app_name='my-chalice-app')

@app.route('/hello')
def hello():
    return {'message': 'Hello from AWS Chalice!'}
```

1. **Run the Local Development Server**: Use the following command to run the local development server:

```bash
bash
Copy code
chalice local
```

1. This command will start a local server, allowing you to test your API endpoint at http://localhost:8000/hello.
2. **Deploy Your Chalice Application**: When you are ready to deploy your application to AWS, use the following command:

```bash
bash
Copy code
chalice deploy
```

1. Chalice will package your application and deploy it to AWS Lambda and API Gateway.

Comparison of Serverless Frameworks

Now that we have explored the main serverless frameworks—Serverless Framework, AWS SAM, and AWS Chalice—let's compare their features, strengths, and use cases to help you determine which framework is right for your project.

FeatureServerless FrameworkAWS SAMAWS Chalice

Language Support

Multi-language support (Node.js, Python, Java, Go, Ruby, etc.)

Primarily for AWS Lambda with multi-language support

Python-centric

Configuration Format

YAML configuration file (serverless.yml)

YAML template file (template.yaml)

Python code

Deployment Complexity

Moderate complexity with extensive configurations

Simple deployment with AWS services

Very simple, mostly automatic deployment

Local Development

Requires additional setup for local testing

Supports local testing via SAM CLI

Built-in local development server

Integration with Cloud Services

Strong multi-provider integration

Deep integration with AWS services

Strong integration with AWS services

Plugins and Extensions

Rich plugin ecosystem

Limited plugins

No external plugins

Best Use Cases

Multi-cloud applications, complex setups

AWS-native applications, cloud formation

Rapid development of Python-based APIs

Choosing the Right Framework for Your Project

When deciding which serverless framework to use, consider the following factors:

1. **Programming Language**: If you primarily work in Python, AWS Chalice is a natural choice due to its focus on Python development. If you prefer a multi-language environment, the Serverless Framework or AWS SAM will suit your needs.

2. **Cloud Provider**: If you are committed to AWS, AWS SAM and AWS

Chalice are excellent options. The Serverless Framework is suitable if you want the flexibility to deploy across multiple cloud providers.

3. **Project Complexity**: For simple applications or APIs, AWS Chalice offers a straightforward approach. For more complex applications that may require extensive configurations, consider using the Serverless Framework or AWS SAM.

4. **Local Development Needs**: If local development is essential for your workflow, AWS SAM provides robust local testing capabilities, while the Serverless Framework supports local development through additional plugins.

5. **Community and Support**: Each framework has a different level of community support and documentation. The Serverless Framework has a large community and extensive documentation, while AWS SAM benefits from AWS's official support.

Conclusion

In this chapter, we explored the world of serverless frameworks, focusing on the Serverless Framework, AWS SAM, and AWS Chalice. Each framework offers unique features and advantages, making them suitable for different use cases and developer preferences. Understanding the capabilities of these frameworks will enable you to choose the right tools for your serverless projects, simplifying the development and deployment processes.

As you continue your serverless journey, consider experimenting with these frameworks to see how they can enhance your development experience. In the next chapter, we will dive deeper into advanced serverless concepts and best practices that will help you build robust, scalable applications.

Chapter 6: Integrating Databases with Serverless

S erverless architecture has gained popularity not only for its ability to abstract infrastructure management but also for its seamless integration with various data storage solutions. Databases play a crucial role in modern applications, serving as the backbone for data persistence, retrieval, and analysis. In this chapter, we will explore how to effectively integrate databases with serverless applications. We will discuss various types of databases suitable for serverless environments, best practices for integration, and real-world examples of how to connect AWS Lambda functions to different database services.

Understanding Database Integration in Serverless Architectures

Integrating databases with serverless applications requires a different approach than traditional architectures. In a serverless context, functions are ephemeral and stateless, meaning they do not maintain persistent connections to databases between invocations. This design necessitates a focus on how data is accessed and managed, as well as how to optimize performance and scalability.

Key Considerations for Database Integration in Serverless

1. **Statelessness**: Serverless functions are designed to be stateless, meaning each function execution is independent. This requires using a connection pooling strategy or establishing new connections during each invocation.

2. **Cold Starts**: When a serverless function is invoked after a period of inactivity, it may experience a cold start, which can introduce latency. This is especially important to consider when connecting to a database, as establishing connections during cold starts may increase response times.

3. **Scalability**: Serverless applications can experience rapid scaling, which can put pressure on databases. It's essential to choose databases that can handle sudden spikes in traffic and scale accordingly.

4. **Data Access Patterns**: Understanding how your application will read and write data is crucial for selecting the right database solution. Depending on the use case, different databases may be more suitable for read-heavy, write-heavy, or mixed workloads.

5. **Cost Management**: Since serverless functions typically incur charges based on execution time and resource usage, it's essential to consider how database access patterns will affect overall costs.

Types of Databases Suitable for Serverless Applications

Several types of databases can be effectively integrated with serverless architectures. Each database type has its advantages and use cases, depending on the application's requirements.

1. NoSQL Databases

NoSQL databases are designed for scalability, flexibility, and performance. They are particularly well-suited for serverless applications due to their ability to handle unstructured data and scale horizontally.

Popular NoSQL Databases:

- **Amazon DynamoDB**: A fully managed NoSQL database service that provides fast and predictable performance with seamless scalability. It supports both key-value and document data models and is commonly used with AWS Lambda.

- **MongoDB Atlas**: A cloud-based database service that provides a managed MongoDB solution. MongoDB is a popular document-oriented NoSQL database that offers flexibility in data modeling.
- **Firebase Firestore**: A NoSQL document database provided by Google that allows for real-time synchronization and offline capabilities, making it ideal for mobile and web applications.

When to Use NoSQL Databases:

- When your application requires high write and read throughput.
- For applications with variable data structures or schemas.
- For applications that need to scale quickly and handle large volumes of data.

2. Relational Databases

Relational databases are structured databases that use tables to store data. They are suitable for applications that require complex queries and transactions.

Popular Relational Databases:

- **Amazon RDS (Relational Database Service)**: A managed relational database service that supports multiple database engines, including MySQL, PostgreSQL, and SQL Server. RDS automates time-consuming tasks such as backups and patching.
- **Aurora Serverless**: A fully managed relational database service that automatically scales based on demand. It combines the benefits of Amazon RDS and serverless architecture, allowing for cost-effective database solutions.
- **Google Cloud SQL**: A fully managed relational database service for MySQL and PostgreSQL on Google Cloud. It offers automated backups, replication, and scalability.

When to Use Relational Databases:

- When your application requires strong consistency and complex querying capabilities.
- For applications that rely heavily on relationships between entities and require ACID compliance.
- When you need to perform complex joins and aggregations on data.

3. In-Memory Databases

In-memory databases are designed to store data in memory for faster access times. They are often used as caching layers to improve performance and reduce latency in serverless applications.

Popular In-Memory Databases:

- **Amazon ElastiCache**: A fully managed caching service that supports Redis and Memcached. It helps improve application performance by providing a high-speed caching layer.
- **Redis**: An open-source in-memory data structure store that can be used as a database, cache, and message broker. It is known for its low-latency performance and support for various data structures.

When to Use In-Memory Databases:

- When you need to reduce latency for frequently accessed data.
- For applications that require fast data retrieval, such as real-time analytics and session management.
- When implementing caching strategies to offload read requests from primary databases.

Integrating AWS Lambda with Databases

In this section, we will focus on integrating AWS Lambda with various databases, specifically Amazon DynamoDB and Amazon RDS. We will provide step-by-step guidance on setting up the necessary configurations and writing code to connect Lambda functions to these databases.

1. Integrating AWS Lambda with Amazon DynamoDB

Amazon DynamoDB is a popular choice for serverless applications due to its managed nature, scalability, and low-latency performance. Here's how to integrate AWS Lambda with DynamoDB.

Step 1: Create a DynamoDB Table

1. **Access DynamoDB**: In the AWS Management Console, navigate to the DynamoDB service.
2. **Create a New Table**: Click on "Create table."
3. **Define Table Settings**:

- **Table Name**: Enter a name for your table (e.g., Users).
- **Primary Key**: Define a primary key. For example, you might use userId as a string type.

1. **Configure Settings**: Leave the default settings for read/write capacity for this tutorial.
2. **Click "Create"**: After configuring the table, click the "Create" button.

Step 2: Update Your Lambda Function to Interact with DynamoDB

1. **Go to Lambda Function**: Navigate to the Lambda function you created earlier (e.g., MyFirstLambdaFunction).
2. **Add DynamoDB Permissions**: In the Lambda console, go to the "Configuration" tab and click on "Permissions." Edit the function's execution role to include permissions for DynamoDB. Attach the policy AmazonDynamoDBFullAccess to allow the function to read and write

to DynamoDB.

3. **Install AWS SDK**: Ensure that the AWS SDK is available in your Lambda environment. For Node.js, the SDK is included by default. For Python, it is also included in the Lambda execution environment.

4. **Modify Your Function Code**: Update the function code to include the logic for interacting with DynamoDB. Here's an example function that adds a user to the DynamoDB table:

```javascript
Copy code
const AWS = require('aws-sdk');
const dynamoDB = new AWS.DynamoDB.DocumentClient();

exports.handler = async (event) => {
    const user = {
        userId: event.userId,
        name: event.name,
        email: event.email,
    };

    const params = {
        TableName: 'Users',
        Item: user,
    };

    try {
        await dynamoDB.put(params).promise();
        return {
            statusCode: 200,
            body: JSON.stringify({ message: 'User added
            successfully!', user }),
        };
    } catch (error) {
        return {
            statusCode: 500,
            body: JSON.stringify({ message: 'Error adding user',
            error }),
```

```
        };
    }
};
```

Step 3: Test Your DynamoDB Integration

1. **Configure a Test Event**: In the Lambda console, create a test event that simulates the data you want to send to the function:

```json
json
Copy code
{
    "userId": "12345",
    "name": "John Doe",
    "email": "john.doe@example.com"
}
```

1. **Run the Test**: Invoke the Lambda function with the test event. You should see a success message indicating that the user was added to the DynamoDB table.
2. **Verify Data in DynamoDB**: Go back to the DynamoDB console, select your Users table, and check the items to verify that the new user has been added.

2. Integrating AWS Lambda with Amazon RDS

Amazon RDS provides managed relational databases that can be integrated with AWS Lambda functions. In this section, we'll demonstrate how to connect a Lambda function to an Amazon RDS MySQL database.

Step 1: Create an RDS Instance

1. **Access RDS**: In the AWS Management Console, navigate to the RDS service.

2. **Create a Database**: Click on "Create database."
3. **Select Engine**: Choose **MySQL** as the database engine.
4. **Choose a Template**: Select the "Free tier" template to stay within the free usage limits.
5. **Configure Settings**: Enter the following configuration details:

- **DB Instance Identifier**: e.g., mydbinstance
- **Master Username**: e.g., admin
- **Master Password**: Choose a secure password.

1. **Configure Database Options**: Keep the default settings for the rest of the configurations and click "Create database."

Step 2: Configure Security Groups

1. **Modify Security Group**: After creating the RDS instance, you need to modify the security group associated with the RDS instance to allow inbound connections from your Lambda function.
2. **Go to EC2 Security Groups**: Navigate to the EC2 service and click on "Security Groups" in the left navigation panel.
3. **Find Your Security Group**: Locate the security group associated with your RDS instance (usually named something like mydbinstance-sg).
4. **Edit Inbound Rules**: Click on the security group and then click "Inbound rules." Add a rule to allow traffic from the Lambda execution role's security group or a specific IP range.

Step 3: Update Your Lambda Function to Connect to RDS

1. **Add RDS Permissions**: In the Lambda console, go to the "Configuration" tab and edit the function's execution role to include permissions for Amazon RDS.
2. **Install MySQL Client**: If your function requires a MySQL client library, you can package it with your deployment package or use a Lambda layer.

3. **Modify Your Function Code**: Update your Lambda function code to connect to the RDS database and execute SQL queries. Here's an example function that retrieves user information from the MySQL database:

```javascript
Copy code
const mysql = require('mysql');

const connection = mysql.createConnection({
    host: 'your-rds-endpoint', // e.g.,
    mydbinstance.abc123xyz.us-west-2.rds.amazonaws.com
    user: 'admin',
    password: 'your-db-password',
    database: 'your-database-name'
});

exports.handler = async (event) => {
    return new Promise((resolve, reject) => {
        connection.query('SELECT * FROM Users WHERE userId = ?',
        [event.userId], (error, results) => {
            if (error) {
                reject({
                    statusCode: 500,
                    body: JSON.stringify({ message: 'Error
                    retrieving user', error }),
                });
            } else {
                resolve({
                    statusCode: 200,
                    body: JSON.stringify(results),
                });
            }
        });
    });
};
```

Step 4: Test Your RDS Integration

1. **Configure a Test Event**: Create a test event in the Lambda console that simulates the data you want to retrieve:

```json
Copy code
{
    "userId": "12345"
}
```

1. **Run the Test**: Invoke the Lambda function with the test event. You should see a success message with the retrieved user information from the MySQL database.
2. **Verify Data in RDS**: Log into the RDS instance using a MySQL client (e.g., MySQL Workbench) and verify the data.

Best Practices for Integrating Databases with Serverless Applications

Integrating databases with serverless applications requires careful consideration of various best practices to ensure performance, reliability, and cost-effectiveness. Here are some essential best practices:

1. Use Connection Pooling

Establishing a new database connection for each invocation can be inefficient, especially with relational databases. Use connection pooling to manage connections more effectively:

- **Connection Pooling Libraries**: Libraries like mysql2 for Node.js support connection pooling out of the box.
- **Keep Connections Open**: Open a connection in the global scope of your function to keep it available across multiple invocations. However, be mindful of the maximum connections your database can handle.

2. Optimize Queries

Performance is critical in serverless applications. Optimize your database queries to minimize response times:

- **Indexing**: Ensure that your database tables are properly indexed to improve query performance.
- **Batch Operations**: When performing multiple write operations, consider using batch inserts or updates to reduce the number of database calls.

3. Handle Timeouts and Retries

In serverless applications, functions may time out if a database operation takes too long. Implement proper timeout handling and retry logic:

- **Set Timeouts**: Set appropriate timeout values for your database connections to avoid hanging requests.
- **Retry Logic**: Implement exponential backoff strategies for retries in case of transient errors or connection issues.

4. Monitor Performance and Errors

Monitoring is crucial for maintaining the health of your serverless applications:

- **CloudWatch**: Use AWS CloudWatch to monitor metrics and logs for both your Lambda functions and databases. Set up alarms to notify you of any performance issues.
- **Database Metrics**: Keep an eye on database metrics such as connection counts, query performance, and latency to identify potential bottlenecks.

5. Consider Data Consistency

In serverless applications, maintaining data consistency is essential, especially in distributed systems:

- **Use Transactions**: For relational databases, leverage transactions to ensure atomicity when performing multiple operations that depend on each other.

- **Eventual Consistency**: In NoSQL databases, understand that some systems provide eventual consistency. Design your application accordingly if you are working with distributed data.

Conclusion

In this chapter, we explored the integration of databases with serverless applications, focusing on Amazon DynamoDB and Amazon RDS. We discussed various types of databases suitable for serverless architectures, the considerations for integration, and best practices to optimize performance and reliability.

Understanding how to effectively integrate databases with serverless applications is crucial for building robust and scalable solutions. By leveraging the strengths of both serverless architecture and managed databases, developers can create applications that meet the demands of modern users while minimizing operational overhead.

In the next chapter, we will delve deeper into best practices for building serverless applications, including how to optimize performance, manage costs, and ensure security in your serverless architecture.

Chapter 7: Optimizing Performance in Serverless

As organizations increasingly adopt serverless architecture, optimizing performance becomes critical to ensuring applications run efficiently and cost-effectively. While serverless computing abstracts away infrastructure management, it introduces unique challenges and considerations that developers must address to achieve optimal performance. This chapter will explore the various strategies for optimizing performance in serverless applications, focusing on reducing latency, minimizing cold starts, managing resources, and implementing best practices for efficient coding and architecture.

Understanding Performance in Serverless Architectures

Performance in serverless environments can be defined by several key metrics:

1. **Latency**: The time it takes for a request to be processed and a response returned. Low latency is crucial for user satisfaction and application responsiveness.
2. **Cold Starts**: The delay that occurs when a serverless function is invoked for the first time after being inactive. Cold starts can significantly

impact performance, particularly for synchronous workflows where users expect immediate feedback.

3. **Execution Time**: The total time taken by a function to execute its code. Optimizing execution time is essential for reducing costs, as serverless billing is often based on the duration of function execution.

4. **Concurrency**: The number of simultaneous requests that a function can handle. Efficiently managing concurrency can prevent throttling and ensure that applications scale appropriately.

5. **Resource Utilization**: The efficient use of resources such as memory and compute power. Underutilization can lead to wasted costs, while overutilization can lead to degraded performance.

The Importance of Performance Optimization

Optimizing performance in serverless applications is crucial for several reasons:

- **Cost Efficiency**: Since serverless platforms often charge based on execution time and resources consumed, optimizing performance can directly lead to reduced operational costs.
- **User Experience**: Applications with high latency or slow response times can lead to poor user experiences, resulting in decreased user engagement and satisfaction.
- **Scalability**: Efficiently optimized applications can handle sudden spikes in traffic without performance degradation, ensuring a consistent experience for users.
- **Reliability**: Optimized serverless applications are less prone to failures caused by resource exhaustion or bottlenecks, enhancing overall system reliability.

Strategies for Optimizing Performance in Serverless

In this section, we will discuss various strategies for optimizing performance in serverless applications, focusing on specific techniques and best practices.

1. Reducing Latency

Latency is a critical metric for serverless applications, as it affects the overall user experience. Here are several strategies to reduce latency:

1.1. Use Provisioned Concurrency

Provisioned concurrency is a feature in AWS Lambda that keeps a specified number of function instances warm and ready to respond immediately to requests. By using provisioned concurrency, you can significantly reduce cold start times, ensuring that your application can handle incoming requests without delays.

- **How to Configure Provisioned Concurrency**:
- In the AWS Lambda console, select your function and navigate to the "Configuration" tab.
- Under the "Concurrency" section, enable provisioned concurrency and specify the desired number of instances.

1.2. Optimize Cold Start Times

To mitigate the impact of cold starts, consider the following practices:

- **Minimize Package Size**: Reducing the size of your deployment package can help decrease cold start times. Use tools like Webpack or Rollup to bundle your code and remove unnecessary dependencies.
- **Keep Dependencies Light**: Avoid including large libraries or frameworks that are not essential for your function. Instead, use lightweight alternatives or only import the necessary parts of a library.
- **Warm-Up Strategies**: Implement a warm-up strategy to periodically invoke your functions, keeping them warm and minimizing the chances of cold starts.

1.3. Optimize Function Code

Efficiently written code can help reduce latency. Consider the following coding practices:

- **Asynchronous Programming**: Use asynchronous programming techniques to handle I/O-bound operations. This allows your function to process multiple requests simultaneously without blocking.
- **Efficient Algorithms**: Optimize algorithms for performance. Choose the right data structures and algorithms that can process data quickly and efficiently.
- **Reduce External API Calls**: Limit the number of external API calls made within your functions. If possible, cache responses or aggregate data to minimize the number of requests.

2. Minimizing Cold Starts

Cold starts can significantly impact serverless applications, particularly those with infrequent invocations. In addition to using provisioned concurrency, here are more strategies to minimize cold starts:

2.1. Monitor and Analyze Cold Start Metrics

Use monitoring tools such as AWS CloudWatch to track cold start occurrences. By analyzing metrics such as invocation duration and cold start times, you can identify patterns and address potential bottlenecks.

2.2. Implement Lambda Layers

Lambda layers allow you to package dependencies separately from your function code, enabling faster cold starts. By placing shared libraries in a layer, your function can quickly access them without bundling them in the deployment package.

- **Creating a Lambda Layer**:
- Package your dependencies in a ZIP file.
- In the AWS Lambda console, create a new layer and upload the ZIP file.
- Associate the layer with your Lambda function.

2.3. Choose the Right Runtime

Different runtimes have varying cold start characteristics. For example, runtimes like Node.js and Python typically have faster cold starts compared to heavier runtimes like Java. When designing your serverless application, choose the runtime that best fits your performance requirements.

3. Managing Resources Effectively

Resource management is crucial for optimizing performance in serverless applications. Here are strategies to manage resources effectively:

3.1. Configure Memory and Timeout Settings

AWS Lambda allows you to configure memory allocation for your functions, which also impacts CPU power. By optimizing memory and timeout settings, you can enhance performance:

- **Memory Allocation**: Experiment with different memory settings to find the optimal configuration for your function. More memory can lead to increased CPU allocation, reducing execution time.
- **Timeout Settings**: Set appropriate timeout values for your functions to prevent them from hanging. Monitor execution times to adjust timeouts accordingly.

3.2. Use Connection Pooling

As discussed earlier, managing database connections is essential for reducing latency. Implement connection pooling to maintain a pool of open connections that can be reused across multiple invocations. This approach helps reduce the overhead of establishing new connections and improves performance.

- **Using Connection Pooling Libraries**: For Node.js, libraries like mysql2 support connection pooling. In Python, libraries such as psycopg2 for PostgreSQL and mysql-connector-python provide similar functionality.

3.3. Leverage Caching

Caching can significantly improve the performance of serverless applications by reducing the need to fetch data repeatedly from databases or external services. Consider implementing caching strategies using services like:

- **Amazon ElastiCache**: A managed caching service that supports Redis and Memcached. Use ElastiCache to cache frequently accessed data and reduce latency.
- **AWS Lambda Caching**: You can also implement in-memory caching within your Lambda functions for short-lived data. However, be mindful that data stored in memory will not persist between function invocations.

3.4. Optimize API Gateway Configuration

If your serverless functions are exposed via API Gateway, optimizing API Gateway configurations can enhance performance:

- **Caching API Responses**: Enable response caching in API Gateway to reduce the load on your Lambda functions and improve response times for frequently accessed endpoints.
- **Regional Endpoints**: Use regional endpoints for your API Gateway to reduce latency for users located in the same region as your Lambda functions.

4. Implementing Best Practices for Efficient Coding

Writing efficient code is vital for optimizing performance in serverless applications. Here are best practices to follow:

4.1. Follow the Single Responsibility Principle

Design your Lambda functions to perform a single task or responsibility. Functions that are too large or complex can lead to longer execution times and increased latency. By following the Single Responsibility Principle, you can create smaller, more focused functions that are easier to manage and optimize.

4.2. Optimize Data Access Patterns

Accessing data efficiently can reduce execution time. Consider the following strategies:

- **Batch Operations**: When interacting with databases, use batch operations to process multiple records in a single call. This can significantly reduce the number of round trips to the database.
- **Avoid Unnecessary Data Retrieval**: Retrieve only the data needed for your application. For example, when querying a database, use selective queries to avoid fetching excessive data.

4.3. Use Environment Variables for Configuration

Using environment variables to manage configuration settings allows you to keep your code clean and flexible. Store sensitive data, such as database connection strings or API keys, in environment variables rather than hardcoding them in your code.

- **Setting Environment Variables in AWS Lambda**:
- In the Lambda console, navigate to your function and click on the "Configuration" tab.
- Scroll down to the "Environment variables" section and add your variables.

4.4. Monitor and Optimize Logs

Logging is essential for debugging and monitoring performance, but excessive logging can introduce latency. Follow these best practices for effective logging:

- **Log Levels**: Use appropriate log levels (e.g., INFO, DEBUG, ERROR) to filter logs based on severity. This allows you to capture necessary information without overwhelming your logging infrastructure.
- **Structured Logging**: Implement structured logging to make it easier to parse and analyze logs. Using formats like JSON can help you capture

contextual information about each log entry.

5. Scaling Serverless Applications

Scaling is a critical aspect of serverless architecture. AWS Lambda automatically scales based on the number of incoming requests, but there are considerations to keep in mind:

5.1. Concurrency Limits

AWS Lambda has default concurrency limits that restrict the number of simultaneous executions of your functions. Understanding these limits is essential for designing scalable applications:

- **Reserved Concurrency**: You can reserve concurrency for specific functions to ensure they have dedicated resources. This is useful for critical functions that require consistent performance.
- **Provisioned Concurrency**: As mentioned earlier, provisioned concurrency keeps a specified number of function instances warm, reducing cold start times and improving responsiveness during peak traffic.

5.2. Design for Scale

Design your serverless applications to handle scaling gracefully:

- **Decoupling Components**: Use event-driven architecture to decouple different components of your application. For example, instead of having a single function handle multiple tasks, create separate functions for each task and use message queues (e.g., SQS or SNS) to communicate between them.
- **Asynchronous Processing**: For long-running tasks, consider using asynchronous processing patterns. Use AWS Step Functions or SQS to queue tasks and process them independently, allowing for better scaling.

5.3. Load Testing

Conduct load testing to understand how your serverless application behaves under different traffic conditions. Use tools like AWS Lambda Power Tuning or third-party solutions to simulate traffic and identify potential bottlenecks.

6. Security Considerations in Serverless Applications

Optimizing performance also involves ensuring that your serverless applications are secure. Here are best practices to consider:

6.1. Use IAM Roles and Policies

AWS Identity and Access Management (IAM) allows you to define roles and policies that determine what actions your Lambda functions can perform and which resources they can access. Follow these practices:

- **Least Privilege Principle**: Grant only the permissions necessary for your function to perform its task. Avoid using overly permissive policies.
- **Use Execution Roles**: Create separate IAM roles for each Lambda function based on its specific permissions. This helps minimize security risks in case of a compromised function.

6.2. Secure Sensitive Data

When working with sensitive data, ensure that you follow best practices for secure storage and transmission:

- **Environment Variables**: Store sensitive information, such as API keys and database credentials, in environment variables instead of hardcoding them in your code.
- **Use Secrets Manager**: Use AWS Secrets Manager to securely store and manage sensitive information. Secrets Manager integrates seamlessly with AWS Lambda and can automatically rotate credentials.

6.3. Implement API Security

If your serverless functions are exposed via API Gateway, ensure that you implement security best practices:

- **Authentication and Authorization**: Use AWS Cognito or API keys to authenticate and authorize users accessing your APIs. Implement OAuth2 or JWT for securing APIs.
- **Rate Limiting**: Enable throttling on API Gateway to limit the number of requests a user can make within a specified time frame. This helps prevent abuse and ensures fair resource usage.

Conclusion

Optimizing performance in serverless applications is a multifaceted challenge that involves various strategies, including reducing latency, minimizing cold starts, managing resources effectively, and implementing best coding practices. By understanding the unique characteristics of serverless architecture and leveraging the right tools and techniques, developers can create high-performing applications that deliver exceptional user experiences.

As you continue your journey into serverless computing, consider the best practices outlined in this chapter to enhance the performance of your applications. In the next chapter, we will explore advanced topics in serverless architecture, including event-driven workflows, API management, and integrating serverless functions with other cloud services. This knowledge will further empower you to build robust and scalable serverless applications.

Chapter 8: Advanced Topics in Serverless Architecture

As you delve deeper into the world of serverless computing, understanding advanced topics becomes crucial for building robust, scalable applications. In this chapter, we will explore various advanced concepts within serverless architecture, including event-driven workflows, API management, integrating serverless functions with other cloud services, best practices for monitoring and logging, and managing costs effectively. Each of these topics will provide you with insights and techniques to enhance your serverless applications' efficiency and performance.

1. Event-Driven Architectures

Event-driven architectures (EDAs) are a core aspect of serverless computing. In an EDA, components communicate with each other through events, allowing systems to react dynamically to changes in state. This decoupling of components enables greater flexibility and scalability in applications.

1.1. Understanding Events

An event is a significant change or action that occurs within a system, which can trigger other actions or workflows. In serverless architectures, events can originate from various sources, such as:

- **User Actions**: Events triggered by user interactions, such as form submissions or button clicks.
- **System Changes**: Changes to data in databases, such as updates, deletions, or insertions.
- **Scheduled Events**: Events triggered by cron-like schedules, such as running a task every hour or day.
- **External Services**: Events generated by third-party services, such as receiving a webhook or message from a message broker.

1.2. Implementing Event-Driven Workflows

Serverless functions can be designed to respond to events from different sources, allowing you to build event-driven workflows. Here's how to implement such workflows:

1.2.1. Using AWS Lambda with Event Sources

AWS Lambda can be triggered by various event sources, including:

- **Amazon S3**: Trigger functions when files are uploaded or deleted in S3 buckets.
- **Amazon DynamoDB**: Trigger functions based on changes to items in DynamoDB tables.
- **Amazon SNS**: Trigger functions in response to notifications sent through the Simple Notification Service (SNS).
- **Amazon SQS**: Trigger functions to process messages in the Simple Queue Service (SQS).

Example Workflow: Consider a scenario where a user uploads an image to an S3 bucket. This event can trigger a Lambda function that processes the image (e.g., resizing or converting formats) and saves the result in another S3 bucket.

1.2.2. Implementing Event-Driven Patterns

To build effective event-driven architectures, consider the following design patterns:

- **Event Sourcing**: Store all changes to application state as a sequence of events, allowing you to reconstruct the current state at any point in time. This pattern enhances auditability and supports complex workflows.
- **CQRS (Command Query Responsibility Segregation)**: Separate the logic for reading data from the logic for writing data. Use events to notify other components of state changes, ensuring that read and write operations are decoupled.
- **Saga Pattern**: Manage distributed transactions by breaking them down into smaller, manageable transactions. Each step in the saga can trigger subsequent actions, ensuring that the overall workflow completes successfully.

1.3. Event-Driven Tools and Services

Several tools and services can help you build and manage event-driven architectures:

- **AWS Step Functions**: A serverless orchestration service that enables you to build workflows by chaining together multiple AWS services and Lambda functions. It provides visual representations of workflows and handles error handling and retries.
- **Apache Kafka**: A distributed event streaming platform that enables the publication, subscription, storage, and processing of streams of records. It is ideal for building real-time data pipelines and event-driven applications.
- **AWS EventBridge**: A serverless event bus service that allows you to connect application data from various sources and route it to target services. It supports event-driven architectures and can integrate with SaaS applications.

2. API Management in Serverless Applications

APIs are the backbone of modern applications, enabling communication between different components and services. In a serverless architecture, managing APIs effectively is essential for delivering high-quality services to users.

2.1. API Gateway Overview

API Gateway is a fully managed service provided by AWS that enables you to create, publish, maintain, and secure APIs. It acts as a single entry point for clients to access backend services, including AWS Lambda functions, microservices, and other resources.

Key Features of API Gateway:

- **Routing and Management**: API Gateway allows you to define RESTful APIs and HTTP endpoints, routing requests to the appropriate backend services based on the request path and method.
- **Rate Limiting and Throttling**: You can configure rate limits and throttling rules to control the number of requests made to your APIs, ensuring that backend services are not overwhelmed.
- **Caching**: API Gateway supports response caching, which can reduce latency and improve performance for frequently accessed endpoints.
- **Security**: You can secure your APIs using AWS Cognito for user authentication, API keys for access control, and resource policies to restrict access based on specific conditions.

2.2. Designing RESTful APIs

When designing APIs for serverless applications, follow RESTful principles to ensure consistency and ease of use:

- **Use Meaningful Resource Names**: Define clear and meaningful resource names that represent the underlying entities in your application. For example, use /users to represent user resources.
- **HTTP Methods**: Use appropriate HTTP methods to represent actions

on resources:
- **GET**: Retrieve data.
- **POST**: Create new resources.
- **PUT/PATCH**: Update existing resources.
- **DELETE**: Remove resources.
- **Status Codes**: Use standard HTTP status codes to convey the outcome of API requests. For example, return 200 OK for successful requests, 404 Not Found for missing resources, and 500 Internal Server Error for server issues.

2.3. API Versioning

As APIs evolve, it's essential to manage versioning to maintain backward compatibility. Here are common strategies for API versioning:

- **URI Versioning**: Include the version number in the API endpoint, such as /v1/users. This method allows clients to specify which version they want to access.
- **Header Versioning**: Use custom headers to specify the API version. Clients can include a header like Accept: application/vnd.myapp.v1+json to indicate their preferred version.
- **Query Parameter Versioning**: Include a version query parameter in the API request, such as /users?version=1. This method can lead to less intuitive URLs, so it is less commonly used.

2.4. Securing APIs

API security is critical to protect your serverless applications from unauthorized access and attacks. Here are best practices for securing your APIs:

- **Authentication and Authorization**: Implement authentication mechanisms such as AWS Cognito to manage user sign-up and sign-in processes. Use token-based authentication (e.g., JWT) for securing API requests.
- **API Keys**: Generate and manage API keys for users or applications accessing your APIs. Use API keys to track usage and limit access based

on user requirements.

- **CORS (Cross-Origin Resource Sharing)**: Configure CORS settings in API Gateway to control which domains can access your API. This helps prevent unauthorized cross-origin requests.
- **Data Validation**: Validate all incoming requests to ensure they meet the expected format and data types. This helps prevent injection attacks and data corruption.

3. Integrating Serverless Functions with Other Cloud Services

Integrating serverless functions with other cloud services is a key aspect of building powerful applications. This section will explore various integration patterns and services that can enhance the capabilities of your serverless applications.

3.1. Connecting to Message Queues

Message queues enable asynchronous communication between different components of your application. They are particularly useful in decoupling services and ensuring reliable message delivery.

Common Message Queues:

- **Amazon SQS (Simple Queue Service)**: A fully managed message queuing service that allows you to decouple microservices and distribute workloads.
- **Amazon SNS (Simple Notification Service)**: A fully managed pub/sub messaging service that enables you to send notifications to multiple subscribers.

Integrating Lambda with SQS and SNS:

- **SQS Integration**: Configure AWS Lambda to poll messages from an SQS queue. Lambda will automatically invoke your function when messages are available, allowing for scalable and reliable processing of queued tasks.

- **SNS Integration**: Use SNS to publish messages to multiple subscribers, including Lambda functions. You can set up your Lambda function to be triggered by SNS notifications, enabling event-driven architectures.

3.2. Interfacing with Storage Services

Serverless applications often require data storage, whether for files, images, or structured data. Integrating storage services with your Lambda functions is essential for handling data efficiently.

Common Storage Services:

- **Amazon S3 (Simple Storage Service)**: A scalable object storage service for storing and retrieving files. It is commonly used to store images, videos, backups, and other unstructured data.
- **Amazon EFS (Elastic File System)**: A managed file storage service that can be mounted to multiple Lambda functions. EFS is useful for sharing data across functions or maintaining persistent storage.

Integrating Lambda with S3 and EFS:

- **S3 Integration**: Configure your Lambda function to be triggered by events in S3, such as file uploads. This allows you to process files automatically upon upload.
- **EFS Integration**: Mount an EFS file system to your Lambda function to access shared file storage. This is useful for applications that require persistent state or file access across multiple invocations.

3.3. Using Databases and Data Lakes

Databases and data lakes are essential for storing structured and unstructured data. Integrating serverless functions with these data storage solutions allows you to build data-driven applications.

Common Data Storage Solutions:

- **Amazon RDS**: A managed relational database service for MySQL,

PostgreSQL, SQL Server, and others.
- **Amazon Redshift**: A managed data warehousing service for large-scale data analytics.
- **Amazon Athena**: An interactive query service that allows you to analyze data in Amazon S3 using standard SQL.

Integrating Lambda with Databases and Data Lakes:

- **RDS Integration**: Use Lambda functions to connect to RDS instances for reading and writing data. Implement connection pooling to manage database connections efficiently.
- **Athena Integration**: Trigger Lambda functions to run SQL queries on data stored in S3 using Athena. This allows you to analyze large datasets without needing to load them into memory.

3.4. Leveraging Third-Party APIs

Serverless applications often need to interact with external services or APIs. Integrating with third-party APIs can enhance the functionality of your applications.

Common Use Cases:

- **Payment Processing**: Integrate with payment gateways (e.g., Stripe, PayPal) to handle transactions within your application.
- **External Data Sources**: Fetch data from external APIs (e.g., weather data, stock prices) to enrich your application's functionality.

Best Practices for API Integration:

- **Error Handling**: Implement robust error handling to manage failures when calling external APIs. Use retries with exponential backoff to handle transient errors.
- **Timeouts**: Set appropriate timeouts for API requests to avoid hanging your Lambda functions. This ensures that your application remains

responsive.

4. Monitoring and Logging in Serverless Applications

Monitoring and logging are essential for maintaining the health and performance of serverless applications. Without proper monitoring, it can be challenging to identify issues, troubleshoot problems, and optimize performance.

4.1. AWS CloudWatch for Monitoring

AWS CloudWatch is a monitoring service that provides insights into AWS resources and applications. It enables you to track metrics, set alarms, and visualize data in real-time.

Key Features of CloudWatch:

- **Metrics**: CloudWatch collects metrics from AWS resources, including Lambda functions, API Gateway, DynamoDB, and more. You can monitor metrics such as invocation count, duration, and error rates.
- **Alarms**: Set up CloudWatch alarms to trigger notifications when specific thresholds are breached. For example, you can create an alarm to notify you when the error rate of a Lambda function exceeds a certain percentage.
- **Dashboards**: Create custom CloudWatch dashboards to visualize key metrics and gain insights into your application's performance. Dashboards can display multiple metrics from different AWS services in one view.

4.2. AWS CloudTrail for Logging

AWS CloudTrail is a service that enables you to log, monitor, and analyze account activity across your AWS infrastructure. It provides a detailed record of API calls made on your account.

Key Features of CloudTrail:

- **Event Logging**: CloudTrail logs all API calls made to AWS services, including Lambda functions and other resources. This allows you to track changes and analyze user activity.

- **Audit Trails**: Use CloudTrail logs to maintain a history of changes made to your AWS environment. This is essential for compliance and auditing purposes.

4.3. Implementing Structured Logging

Structured logging helps improve the quality and usability of your logs. By capturing logs in a structured format (e.g., JSON), you can easily parse and analyze log data.

Best Practices for Structured Logging:

- **Include Contextual Information**: Capture relevant context in your logs, such as request IDs, user IDs, and timestamps. This information helps in troubleshooting and correlating logs with specific requests.
- **Log Levels**: Use appropriate log levels (e.g., INFO, WARN, ERROR) to classify the severity of log messages. This enables you to filter logs based on importance.
- **Log Aggregation**: Use log aggregation tools like AWS CloudWatch Logs Insights or third-party services (e.g., ELK Stack, Splunk) to collect and analyze logs from multiple sources.

5. Managing Costs in Serverless Architectures

While serverless computing can be cost-effective, managing costs requires careful planning and monitoring. In this section, we will discuss strategies for managing costs effectively in serverless architectures.

5.1. Understanding Pricing Models

Serverless platforms often use pay-as-you-go pricing models, charging based on resource usage, such as compute time, memory allocation, and the number of requests. Understanding these pricing models is crucial for managing costs effectively.

- **AWS Lambda Pricing**: AWS Lambda charges based on the number of requests (in millions) and the duration of code execution (measured in milliseconds). Additionally, memory allocation affects execution time.
- **API Gateway Pricing**: API Gateway charges based on the number of API calls and data transfer out. Understanding the pricing model helps you estimate costs based on expected usage.

5.2. Monitoring and Analyzing Costs

Use AWS Cost Explorer and CloudWatch to monitor and analyze costs associated with your serverless applications:

- **Cost Explorer**: This tool allows you to visualize and analyze your AWS spending. Set up cost allocation tags to track spending by individual services or applications.
- **CloudWatch Metrics**: Monitor metrics related to resource usage, such as invocation count and execution duration. This information can help you identify trends and optimize resource allocation.

5.3. Implementing Cost Optimization Strategies

To manage costs effectively, consider implementing the following strategies:

- **Right-Sizing Resources**: Regularly review your Lambda function configurations, including memory allocation and timeout settings. Right-size resources based on actual usage patterns to avoid over-provisioning.
- **Optimize Code**: Efficiently written code can reduce execution time and costs. Follow best practices for coding, such as optimizing algorithms and minimizing external API calls.
- **Use Caching**: Implement caching strategies to reduce the number of database calls and API requests, ultimately lowering operational costs.
- **Leverage the Free Tier**: Take advantage of the free tier offered by AWS for services like Lambda and API Gateway. Monitor your usage to ensure you stay within the free limits.

- **Scheduled Tasks**: Use scheduled tasks to invoke Lambda functions only when needed, reducing unnecessary invocations and costs.

6. Case Studies: Real-World Applications of Serverless Architecture

Understanding real-world applications of serverless architecture can provide insights into best practices and effective implementation strategies. In this section, we will explore a few case studies of companies successfully utilizing serverless technologies.

Case Study 1: Netflix

Overview: Netflix, the popular streaming service, uses serverless architecture to handle various tasks, including encoding video, generating thumbnails, and processing user interactions.

Implementation:

- **Lambda for Video Processing**: Netflix uses AWS Lambda functions to process videos uploaded by users. The serverless architecture enables quick and scalable video encoding without managing servers.
- **Event-Driven Workflows**: Lambda functions are triggered by S3 events when new videos are uploaded. This allows for real-time processing and improves user experience.

Results:

- **Scalability**: The serverless architecture allows Netflix to scale effortlessly based on demand, accommodating millions of users without performance degradation.
- **Cost Savings**: By leveraging serverless technologies, Netflix reduces infrastructure costs while ensuring efficient resource utilization.

Case Study 2: Coca-Cola

Overview: Coca-Cola implemented serverless architecture to streamline its marketing campaigns and manage data from various sources.

Implementation:

- **Data Aggregation**: Coca-Cola uses AWS Lambda to aggregate data from multiple sources, including social media, sales data, and customer feedback.
- **Real-Time Analytics**: The serverless architecture enables real-time analytics to monitor campaign performance and customer sentiment.

Results:

- **Enhanced Decision-Making**: The ability to analyze data in real time allows Coca-Cola to make data-driven decisions quickly, improving marketing effectiveness.
- **Reduced Time to Market**: By automating data processing and analysis, Coca-Cola accelerates the time it takes to launch new marketing campaigns.

Case Study 3: Nordstrom

Overview: Nordstrom, a leading fashion retailer, utilizes serverless architecture to enhance its e-commerce platform and improve customer experience.

Implementation:

- **Personalized Recommendations**: Nordstrom employs AWS Lambda functions to generate personalized product recommendations for customers based on browsing history and preferences.
- **API Integration**: Serverless functions interact with external APIs to fetch product data, availability, and pricing information.

Results:

- **Improved User Experience**: The serverless architecture allows Nordstrom to provide personalized shopping experiences, increasing customer engagement and sales.

- **Efficient Resource Management**: By leveraging serverless technologies, Nordstrom minimizes operational overhead and focuses on enhancing the customer experience.

Conclusion

In this chapter, we explored advanced topics in serverless architecture,
including event-driven workflows, API management, integration with other
cloud services, monitoring and logging, and managing costs effectively.
Understanding these concepts is essential for building scalable, efficient
serverless applications that meet the demands of modern users.

As you continue your journey into serverless computing, consider the
strategies and best practices discussed in this chapter to optimize your
applications. In the next chapter, we will delve into security considerations
in serverless architecture, exploring how to protect your applications and
data in a cloud environment. This knowledge will equip you with the tools
necessary to build secure and resilient serverless applications.

Chapter 9: Security in Serverless Architectures

A s organizations increasingly adopt serverless architectures, the importance of security cannot be overstated. Serverless computing offers many advantages, such as reduced operational overhead and automatic scaling, but it also introduces unique security challenges. In this chapter, we will explore the various security considerations and best practices associated with serverless architectures. We will discuss topics such as identity and access management, securing serverless functions, protecting data in transit and at rest, monitoring for threats, and compliance considerations.

1. Understanding the Security Model of Serverless Computing

Before diving into specific security practices, it's essential to understand the underlying security model of serverless architectures.

1.1. Shared Responsibility Model

In serverless computing, the shared responsibility model defines the security responsibilities of both the cloud provider and the customer. In this model:

- **Cloud Provider Responsibilities**: The cloud provider is responsible for securing the underlying infrastructure, including servers, storage, and networking. This includes patching vulnerabilities, securing physical data centers, and managing the security of services such as AWS Lambda, Azure Functions, and Google Cloud Functions.

- **Customer Responsibilities**: Customers are responsible for securing their applications, data, and identity management. This includes configuring permissions, implementing security best practices, and managing data privacy.

Understanding this model is crucial for effectively managing security in serverless applications.

1.2. Unique Security Challenges in Serverless Architectures

While serverless architectures simplify many aspects of application development, they also introduce specific security challenges, including:

- **Increased Attack Surface**: With multiple functions and services interacting, the number of potential attack vectors increases. Each function and API endpoint can become a target for attacks.
- **Ephemeral Nature of Functions**: Serverless functions are stateless and ephemeral, which can complicate traditional security measures. For example, managing persistent connections and state can be challenging in a serverless environment.
- **Third-Party Dependencies**: Serverless applications often rely on third-party services and libraries. Vulnerabilities in these dependencies can expose your application to risks.
- **Data Privacy**: Ensuring data privacy in transit and at rest is critical. Organizations must implement robust measures to protect sensitive data from unauthorized access.

2. Identity and Access Management (IAM)

Effective identity and access management is crucial for securing serverless applications. AWS IAM, Azure Active Directory, and similar services provide mechanisms to control access to resources.

2.1. Principles of Least Privilege

The principle of least privilege states that users and services should have only the permissions necessary to perform their tasks. This principle helps reduce the potential impact of security breaches.

Best Practices for Implementing Least Privilege:

- **Define Fine-Grained Permissions**: Use fine-grained IAM policies to specify exactly which actions are allowed for each user or service. Avoid overly broad permissions that grant access to unnecessary resources.
- **Regularly Review IAM Policies**: Conduct regular audits of IAM policies to ensure that they are still relevant and enforce the principle of least privilege.
- **Use Role-Based Access Control (RBAC)**: Implement role-based access control to group permissions by roles rather than individual users. This simplifies permission management and enforces consistent access controls.

2.2. Using IAM Roles for Serverless Functions

In serverless architectures, functions often require access to other AWS services. Instead of embedding credentials directly in your code, use IAM roles to grant permissions:

- **Create IAM Roles for Lambda Functions**: When creating a Lambda function, assign it an IAM role with the necessary permissions to access resources like DynamoDB, S3, or SNS.
- **Temporary Credentials**: AWS automatically provides temporary credentials to Lambda functions when they assume an IAM role. This eliminates the need for long-lived credentials in your code.

2.3. Secure API Access

When exposing APIs, it's essential to secure access to those endpoints. Here are some best practices:

- **API Keys**: Use API keys to restrict access to your APIs. Generate unique keys for each client or application and monitor usage for unusual patterns.
- **Authentication and Authorization**: Implement authentication mechanisms such as AWS Cognito or OAuth2 to verify user identities and authorize access to APIs.

3. Securing Serverless Functions

Securing the serverless functions themselves is paramount to protecting your application. Here are various practices to enhance the security of your functions.

3.1. Code Security Practices

Writing secure code is fundamental to preventing vulnerabilities in serverless functions. Consider the following practices:

- **Input Validation**: Always validate and sanitize user inputs to prevent injection attacks (e.g., SQL injection, command injection). Use libraries that provide robust input validation mechanisms.
- **Dependency Management**: Regularly update and manage dependencies to ensure you are using the latest, most secure versions of libraries and frameworks.
- **Static Code Analysis**: Use static code analysis tools to identify potential vulnerabilities in your code during the development process. Tools such as Snyk and Checkmarx can help detect issues early.

3.2. Implementing Environment Variables Securely

Serverless functions often require access to configuration settings and sensitive information. Use environment variables to manage these securely:

- **Store Sensitive Data in Environment Variables**: Use environment variables to store sensitive information, such as database connection strings and API keys, instead of hardcoding them in your code.
- **Encrypt Sensitive Variables**: Consider encrypting sensitive data before storing it in environment variables. For AWS, you can use AWS Secrets Manager or AWS KMS (Key Management Service) to encrypt secrets.

3.3. Logging and Monitoring

Logging is essential for detecting and responding to security incidents. Implement logging best practices for your serverless functions:

- **Structured Logging**: Use structured logging (e.g., JSON format) to capture contextual information about each invocation. This makes it easier to analyze logs and detect anomalies.
- **Centralized Log Management**: Use centralized log management services (e.g., AWS CloudWatch Logs, ELK Stack) to aggregate logs from all your serverless functions. This enables better visibility and correlation of events.

4. Protecting Data in Transit and at Rest

Data security is paramount in serverless architectures. Protecting data both in transit and at rest is crucial to ensuring privacy and compliance.

4.1. Encrypting Data in Transit

To protect data in transit, implement the following measures:

- **Use HTTPS**: Always use HTTPS for APIs to encrypt data transmitted between clients and your serverless functions. AWS API Gateway automatically provides HTTPS endpoints.
- **Secure WebSockets**: If your application uses WebSockets for real-time communication, ensure that you use secure WebSocket (WSS) connections.

4.2. Encrypting Data at Rest

Data stored in databases and storage services should be encrypted to prevent unauthorized access:

- **AWS Encryption Services**: AWS provides various encryption services to secure data at rest. Use Amazon S3 server-side encryption (SSE) for S3 buckets and enable encryption for RDS instances and DynamoDB tables.
- **Key Management**: Use AWS KMS to manage encryption keys securely. KMS enables you to create and control the encryption keys used to encrypt your data.

5. Monitoring for Threats

Continuous monitoring is essential for detecting and responding to security threats in serverless applications.

5.1. Real-Time Threat Detection

Implement real-time threat detection mechanisms to identify potential security incidents as they occur:

- **AWS CloudTrail**: Use AWS CloudTrail to monitor API calls made to AWS services. Analyze CloudTrail logs to detect unusual or unauthorized activities.
- **Amazon GuardDuty**: Enable Amazon GuardDuty, a threat detection service that continuously monitors for malicious activity and unauthorized behavior across your AWS accounts.

5.2. Implementing Intrusion Detection Systems

Intrusion detection systems (IDS) can help identify suspicious activity within your serverless applications:

- **Network Security**: Use AWS services like VPC Flow Logs to monitor network traffic patterns and detect anomalies.
- **Lambda Layer for Security Monitoring**: Consider implementing a

Lambda layer that includes security monitoring tools. This allows you to enhance your serverless functions with security capabilities without modifying the core function code.

6. Compliance Considerations in Serverless Architectures

Compliance is a critical aspect of security, particularly for organizations that handle sensitive data or are subject to regulatory requirements. In this section, we will explore considerations for achieving compliance in serverless architectures.

6.1. Understanding Compliance Frameworks

Familiarize yourself with relevant compliance frameworks and regulations that may apply to your organization, such as:

- **GDPR**: The General Data Protection Regulation outlines data protection and privacy requirements for organizations operating in the European Union.
- **HIPAA**: The Health Insurance Portability and Accountability Act sets standards for protecting sensitive patient health information in the healthcare sector.
- **PCI DSS**: The Payment Card Industry Data Security Standard establishes security requirements for organizations handling credit card information.

6.2. Conducting Risk Assessments

Regularly conduct risk assessments to identify potential security vulnerabilities and compliance gaps within your serverless applications:

- **Identify Sensitive Data**: Catalog sensitive data stored or processed by your applications and assess the risks associated with that data.
- **Evaluate Third-Party Services**: Assess the security posture of third-party services and APIs integrated into your serverless architecture.

6.3. Implementing Auditing and Reporting

Implement auditing and reporting mechanisms to ensure compliance with security policies and regulations:

- **Automated Reporting**: Use automated tools to generate compliance reports and track security metrics. This helps streamline the auditing process and provides visibility into your security posture.
- **Regular Audits**: Schedule regular audits of your serverless applications to assess compliance with security policies and regulatory requirements.

Chapter 10: Best Practices for Building Serverless Applications

A serverless computing continues to evolve, adopting best practices becomes essential for building efficient, scalable, and maintainable applications. This chapter explores various best practices for developing serverless applications, including architecture design principles, deployment strategies, performance optimization, security measures, and effective monitoring and logging. By following these best practices, developers can enhance their serverless applications' quality, reliability, and overall performance.

1. Architectural Design Principles

1.1. Design for Scalability

When building serverless applications, it is crucial to design for scalability from the outset. Serverless platforms inherently provide auto-scaling capabilities, but your application design should consider how components interact under varying loads.

- **Decouple Components**: Use event-driven architectures to decouple different components of your application. This approach allows each component to scale independently based on demand.

- **Microservices Architecture**: Break your application into microservices that handle specific tasks. Each service can be developed, deployed, and scaled independently, leading to better resource utilization.
- **Horizontal Scaling**: Design your serverless functions to handle concurrent executions efficiently. Ensure that your functions are stateless and can be invoked simultaneously without dependencies on shared state.

1.2. Embrace Event-Driven Patterns

Event-driven architectures are a natural fit for serverless applications, allowing for more flexibility and responsiveness.

- **Use Event Sources**: Integrate your serverless functions with event sources such as AWS S3, DynamoDB Streams, and SNS. This enables your application to respond to changes in real time.
- **Implement Workflow Automation**: Use tools like AWS Step Functions to coordinate workflows across multiple functions and services. This helps manage complex processes and ensures that tasks are completed in the correct order.
- **Adopt Publish/Subscribe Models**: Implement publish/subscribe messaging patterns to facilitate communication between components without direct dependencies. This enhances decoupling and allows for easier scaling.

1.3. Focus on Statelessness

Serverless functions are inherently stateless, meaning they do not maintain any state between invocations.

- **Avoid In-Memory State**: Do not rely on in-memory state, as it will not persist between function executions. Instead, use external data stores (e.g., databases, caches) to maintain application state.
- **Leverage Persistent Storage**: Store application state and user data in services like DynamoDB, S3, or RDS. Ensure that your functions can read from and write to these storage services as needed.

- **Utilize Distributed Caching**: For frequently accessed data, consider using caching services like Amazon ElastiCache to reduce latency and improve performance while maintaining statelessness.

2. Effective Deployment Strategies

2.1. Use Infrastructure as Code (IaC)

Infrastructure as Code allows you to manage your serverless resources using code, providing consistency and repeatability.

- **Tools and Frameworks**: Use tools like AWS CloudFormation, AWS SAM, or the Serverless Framework to define your infrastructure as code. This allows you to version control your infrastructure alongside your application code.
- **Automated Deployments**: Implement CI/CD pipelines to automate the deployment of your serverless applications. This ensures that changes are deployed consistently and minimizes the risk of human error.

2.2. Versioning and Rollbacks

Versioning is essential for managing changes to your serverless functions and APIs.

- **Lambda Function Versions**: Use versioning in AWS Lambda to create immutable versions of your functions. This allows you to deploy updates without affecting existing users.
- **API Gateway Stages**: Utilize API Gateway stages to manage different versions of your APIs. This enables you to deploy changes to a staging environment before promoting them to production.
- **Rollback Strategies**: Implement rollback strategies to revert to a previous version of a function or API if issues arise after deployment. This helps maintain application stability during updates.

2.3. Continuous Integration and Continuous Deployment (CI/CD)

Implementing CI/CD practices is essential for ensuring that your serverless applications are deployed efficiently and reliably.

- **Automated Testing**: Integrate automated testing into your CI/CD pipeline to catch bugs early in the development process. Use unit tests, integration tests, and end-to-end tests to validate your application.
- **Canary Deployments**: Use canary deployments to gradually roll out changes to a small percentage of users before deploying to the entire user base. This allows you to monitor performance and quickly identify issues.
- **Blue/Green Deployments**: Implement blue/green deployments to minimize downtime during releases. This strategy involves maintaining two separate environments (blue and green) and switching traffic between them during updates.

3. Performance Optimization Techniques

3.1. Optimize Function Configuration

Configuring your serverless functions correctly can lead to significant performance improvements.

- **Memory Allocation**: Experiment with different memory settings to find the optimal configuration for your functions. Increasing memory allocation can lead to faster execution times, as AWS Lambda allocates more CPU power with higher memory settings.
- **Timeout Settings**: Set appropriate timeout values for your functions based on expected execution times. This helps avoid unnecessary timeouts while ensuring functions do not run indefinitely.

3.2. Minimize Cold Starts

Cold starts can introduce latency in serverless applications. Here are strategies to minimize their impact:

- **Provisioned Concurrency**: Use provisioned concurrency to keep a specified number of function instances warm and ready to respond to requests instantly.
- **Optimize Package Size**: Reduce the size of your deployment package by including only essential libraries and dependencies. This helps minimize the time required to load the function.
- **Choose Lighter Runtimes**: Select runtimes known for faster cold start times, such as Node.js or Python, if suitable for your application.

3.3. Caching Strategies

Implement caching strategies to reduce the load on your backend services and improve response times.

- **API Caching**: Use caching at the API Gateway level to cache responses for frequently accessed endpoints. This reduces the number of calls made to your Lambda functions.
- **Database Caching**: Implement caching solutions such as Amazon ElastiCache to cache database query results. This minimizes database access times and reduces costs.

4. Security Best Practices

Security is a critical consideration in serverless applications. Here are best practices to enhance security:

4.1. Secure Your Functions

Implement measures to secure your serverless functions and their code.

- **Code Security**: Follow secure coding practices, including input validation, sanitization, and using well-maintained libraries.
- **Dependency Management**: Regularly update and audit dependencies to ensure that vulnerabilities are addressed.
- **Static Code Analysis**: Use static code analysis tools to identify security vulnerabilities in your codebase before deployment.

4.2. IAM Policies and Roles

Manage access to your serverless resources effectively.

- **Use Least Privilege**: Grant only the permissions necessary for your functions to perform their tasks. Avoid using overly permissive IAM policies.
- **Role-Based Access Control (RBAC)**: Use RBAC to group permissions based on roles, simplifying management and reducing security risks.
- **Temporary Credentials**: Use temporary credentials for accessing other AWS services, avoiding long-lived credentials in your code.

4.3. Secure Data Handling

Protect sensitive data throughout your application lifecycle.

- **Encryption**: Use encryption to protect sensitive data both in transit (HTTPS) and at rest (encryption services like AWS KMS).
- **Environment Variables**: Store sensitive information in environment variables instead of hardcoding it in your functions.

5. Monitoring and Observability

Effective monitoring and observability practices are essential for maintaining the health of your serverless applications.

5.1. CloudWatch for Monitoring

AWS CloudWatch provides comprehensive monitoring capabilities for serverless applications.

- **Metrics and Alarms**: Set up CloudWatch metrics to monitor function invocations, duration, error rates, and throttling. Create alarms to notify you of any anomalies.
- **Custom Dashboards**: Create custom dashboards in CloudWatch to visualize key performance metrics and gain insights into application behavior.

5.2. Centralized Logging

Centralized logging helps you track application behavior and troubleshoot issues effectively.

- **CloudWatch Logs**: Use CloudWatch Logs to aggregate logs from all your Lambda functions. Implement structured logging to make log analysis easier.
- **Log Analysis Tools**: Consider using log analysis tools like AWS Cloud-Watch Logs Insights, ELK Stack, or Splunk for advanced querying and visualization.

5.3. Distributed Tracing

Distributed tracing enables you to trace requests across multiple services and functions.

- **AWS X-Ray**: Integrate AWS X-Ray with your serverless applications to visualize the flow of requests through different components. This helps identify bottlenecks and optimize performance.
- **Third-Party Tracing Solutions**: Consider using third-party distributed tracing solutions like Datadog or New Relic for enhanced observability across your application stack.

6. Cost Management Strategies

While serverless architectures can reduce operational costs, managing costs effectively is crucial.

6.1. Understand Pricing Models

Familiarize yourself with the pricing models of the services you use in your serverless applications.

- **AWS Lambda Pricing**: Understand how AWS Lambda charges based on the number of requests and execution duration. Monitor your usage to identify cost trends.

- **API Gateway Pricing**: Keep track of the number of API calls made through API Gateway and adjust usage patterns accordingly.

6.2. Monitor and Analyze Costs

Use AWS Cost Explorer and CloudWatch to monitor costs associated with your serverless applications.

- **Cost Explorer**: Analyze your spending patterns over time and identify any unexpected costs.
- **Tagging Resources**: Implement tagging for your AWS resources to track costs by project, environment, or application.

6.3. Optimize Resource Usage

Adopt strategies to optimize resource usage and reduce costs:

- **Right-Sizing Resources**: Regularly review function configurations, including memory and timeout settings, to ensure they match your application's needs.
- **Caching**: Implement caching strategies to reduce database and API call costs.
- **Scheduled Functions**: Use scheduled functions (e.g., via CloudWatch Events) to invoke functions only when necessary, minimizing unnecessary executions.

7. Case Studies: Best Practices in Action

Examining real-world applications of serverless best practices can provide valuable insights.

Case Study 1: Spotify

Overview: Spotify, the popular music streaming service, leverages serverless architecture to enhance its data processing capabilities.

Implementation:

- **Data Ingestion**: Spotify uses AWS Lambda to process millions of events from user interactions in real time. Each user action triggers a Lambda function to analyze and store data in AWS S3 and DynamoDB.
- **Event-Driven Workflows**: Spotify implements an event-driven architecture that allows it to scale processing based on user activity, optimizing resource usage.

Results:

- **Improved User Experience**: By processing data in real time, Spotify can provide personalized recommendations and enhance user engagement.
- **Cost Efficiency**: The serverless architecture allows Spotify to handle fluctuating user loads without overprovisioning resources.

Case Study 2: Expedia

Overview: Expedia, a leading online travel agency, uses serverless computing to streamline its booking processes and improve customer experience.

Implementation:

- **Dynamic Pricing**: Expedia employs AWS Lambda to adjust pricing dynamically based on user demand and market trends. Functions are triggered by changes in inventory and user behavior.
- **API Gateway for Booking Services**: Expedia uses API Gateway to manage its booking APIs, allowing seamless integration with backend services and ensuring scalability.

Results:

- **Enhanced Scalability**: Expedia's serverless architecture enables it to handle peak travel seasons without performance degradation.
- **Faster Development Cycles**: By adopting serverless technologies, Expedia accelerates the development of new features and services.

8. Conclusion

In this chapter, we explored best practices for building serverless applications, including architectural design principles, effective deployment strategies, performance optimization techniques, security measures, and monitoring practices. Understanding and implementing these best practices is essential for developing high-quality, scalable, and secure serverless applications.

As you continue to build and optimize your serverless applications, consider the insights and strategies discussed in this chapter. In the next chapter, we will delve into future trends and innovations in serverless computing, exploring how emerging technologies and practices will shape the evolution of serverless architectures. This knowledge will equip you with a forward-looking perspective as you navigate the rapidly changing landscape of serverless computing.

Chapter 11: Future Trends in Serverless Computing

As serverless computing continues to evolve, new trends and innovations are emerging that will shape the future of this architecture. These trends include advancements in technology, the integration of artificial intelligence (AI) and machine learning (ML), increased focus on security and compliance, and the growing adoption of multi-cloud strategies. In this chapter, we will explore these future trends in serverless computing, discussing how they will impact development practices, application design, and overall business strategies.

1. The Rise of Event-Driven Architectures

1.1. Understanding Event-Driven Architectures

Event-driven architectures (EDAs) are gaining prominence in serverless computing due to their ability to create responsive and scalable applications. In an event-driven model, applications react to events generated by user actions, system changes, or external sources, enabling real-time processing and automation.

1.2. The Growth of Serverless Event Sources

As organizations increasingly adopt serverless architectures, the demand for event-driven capabilities is on the rise. Major cloud providers are expanding their offerings of event sources, making it easier for developers to build event-driven applications.

- **Integration with IoT**: With the proliferation of Internet of Things (IoT) devices, serverless architectures will increasingly leverage events generated by these devices. For example, AWS IoT can trigger Lambda functions based on sensor readings or device state changes.
- **Improved Workflow Automation**: Services like AWS Step Functions and Azure Logic Apps will enable developers to design complex workflows that respond to events from various sources, streamlining processes and enhancing productivity.

1.3. Implications for Development Practices

The rise of event-driven architectures will significantly influence development practices:

- **Focus on Microservices**: Developers will increasingly adopt microservices architectures to create modular, event-driven applications. This approach allows for independent scaling and deployment of services based on event patterns.
- **Enhanced Responsiveness**: Event-driven applications will enable organizations to respond quickly to changes in user behavior, market conditions, and operational requirements, leading to improved customer satisfaction.

2. Integration of Artificial Intelligence and Machine Learning

2.1. Leveraging AI and ML in Serverless Applications

The integration of artificial intelligence (AI) and machine learning (ML) into serverless computing is poised to revolutionize application development. Serverless architectures provide an efficient and scalable environment for running AI and ML models without the need for managing infrastructure.

2.2. Serverless AI and ML Services

Major cloud providers are introducing serverless services specifically designed for AI and ML:

- **AWS SageMaker**: AWS SageMaker offers a fully managed service for building, training, and deploying machine learning models. Developers can integrate SageMaker with AWS Lambda to invoke models in response to events, making it easier to implement real-time predictions.
- **Azure Functions with Azure Machine Learning**: Microsoft Azure enables developers to use Azure Functions to trigger ML models and perform predictions in real time. This integration simplifies the deployment of intelligent applications.
- **Google Cloud Functions with AI Platform**: Google Cloud allows developers to use Cloud Functions to invoke AI models hosted on the AI Platform, providing serverless access to powerful machine learning capabilities.

2.3. Use Cases for AI and ML in Serverless

The integration of AI and ML into serverless applications enables a wide range of use cases:

- **Real-Time Data Processing**: Serverless functions can process data streams from IoT devices, analyze the data using machine learning models, and generate real-time insights.
- **Chatbots and Virtual Assistants**: Serverless architectures can support chatbots and virtual assistants by invoking AI models to understand and respond to user queries.
- **Predictive Analytics**: Organizations can build predictive analytics applications that leverage serverless functions to analyze historical data and forecast future trends.

3. Focus on Security and Compliance

3.1. Increasing Emphasis on Security

As serverless computing matures, security remains a top concern for organizations. With the rise of cyber threats, securing serverless applications will require ongoing vigilance and investment.

3.2. Advanced Security Tools and Services

Cloud providers are enhancing their security offerings to address the unique challenges of serverless architectures:

- **Serverless Security Frameworks**: Frameworks such as AWS Lambda Power Tuning and Serverless Framework Security can help developers analyze and improve the security posture of their applications.
- **Automated Security Audits**: Tools that automatically audit serverless applications for vulnerabilities and compliance issues will become more prevalent, enabling organizations to identify and address risks quickly.

3.3. Compliance Automation

With increasing regulatory requirements, organizations will seek to automate compliance processes in their serverless applications:

- **Automated Compliance Checks**: Cloud providers will introduce tools that automatically check for compliance with industry standards and regulations (e.g., GDPR, HIPAA).
- **Audit Trails**: Enhanced logging and auditing capabilities will allow organizations to maintain comprehensive records of access and changes to serverless resources, facilitating compliance efforts.

4. Multi-Cloud Strategies

4.1. The Shift Towards Multi-Cloud Environments

Organizations are increasingly adopting multi-cloud strategies to avoid vendor lock-in, enhance resilience, and optimize costs. Serverless computing fits well into this trend, as many cloud providers offer serverless solutions.

4.2. Advantages of Multi-Cloud Approaches

- **Flexibility**: Organizations can choose the best services from multiple cloud providers to meet their specific needs, enhancing flexibility and adaptability.
- **Disaster Recovery**: Multi-cloud architectures improve disaster recovery capabilities by ensuring that applications can failover to another cloud provider if one experiences outages.
- **Cost Optimization**: By leveraging multiple cloud providers, organizations can optimize costs based on usage patterns and pricing models.

4.3. Best Practices for Multi-Cloud Serverless Architectures

To implement effective multi-cloud serverless architectures, organizations should consider the following best practices:

- **Standardization**: Establish standard practices for deploying and managing serverless applications across multiple cloud providers to ensure consistency and reduce complexity.
- **Interoperability**: Leverage open standards and APIs to enable interoperability between different cloud services, allowing seamless communication between functions and services.
- **Monitoring and Management Tools**: Use monitoring and management tools that provide visibility across multi-cloud environments, allowing organizations to track performance and resource utilization effectively.

5. Enhanced Monitoring and Observability

5.1. The Need for Comprehensive Monitoring

As serverless applications become more complex, the need for comprehensive monitoring and observability is paramount. Organizations must gain insights into application performance, user behavior, and potential issues.

5.2. Advanced Monitoring Solutions

Cloud providers are developing advanced monitoring solutions tailored for serverless applications:

- **Real-Time Dashboards**: Organizations can create real-time dashboards that visualize key performance metrics and logs from serverless functions and other cloud services.
- **Distributed Tracing**: Tools like AWS X-Ray and OpenTelemetry allow organizations to implement distributed tracing, enabling them to follow requests as they move through various services and functions.

5.3. Proactive Incident Management

Proactive incident management involves identifying and addressing issues before they impact users:

- **Automated Alerts**: Set up automated alerts for critical performance thresholds and anomalies in application behavior, allowing teams to respond quickly.
- **Incident Response Plans**: Develop and implement incident response plans that outline steps to take when an issue is detected, ensuring quick resolution and minimal downtime.

6. Serverless Frameworks and Tools

6.1. Evolving Serverless Frameworks

Serverless frameworks are continually evolving to meet the demands of developers and organizations. New tools and enhancements will emerge to simplify development and deployment processes.

6.2. Key Trends in Serverless Frameworks

- **Integration with CI/CD Pipelines**: Serverless frameworks will increasingly integrate with CI/CD tools, streamlining deployment processes and enabling rapid iterations.
- **Support for Multiple Languages**: As the developer community grows,

serverless frameworks will expand their support for multiple programming languages and runtimes.

- **Enhanced Local Development Environments**: Frameworks will provide better local development environments to enable developers to test and debug functions without deploying to the cloud.

7. Sustainable Serverless Computing

7.1. The Importance of Sustainability

As organizations become more aware of their environmental impact, sustainable computing practices will gain traction in the serverless ecosystem.

7.2. Energy Efficiency in Serverless Architectures

Serverless architectures inherently promote energy efficiency by optimizing resource utilization. However, organizations can take additional steps to enhance sustainability:

- **Resource Management**: Implement efficient resource management practices to reduce waste and minimize energy consumption.
- **Sustainable Cloud Providers**: Choose cloud providers that prioritize sustainability and invest in renewable energy sources for their data centers.

7.3. Measuring Carbon Footprint

Organizations will increasingly seek ways to measure the carbon footprint of their serverless applications. This will involve tracking energy usage and emissions associated with cloud resources.

8. Conclusion

In this chapter, we explored the future trends in serverless computing, including the rise of event-driven architectures, the integration of AI and ML, the focus on security and compliance, multi-cloud strategies, enhanced monitoring and observability, evolving serverless frameworks, and the importance of sustainability. These trends will significantly impact how organizations design, develop, and deploy serverless applications in the coming years.

As you navigate the rapidly changing landscape of serverless computing, staying informed about these trends and adopting best practices will be essential for building successful, resilient, and secure serverless applications. In the next chapter, we will discuss practical case studies of organizations successfully leveraging serverless architectures, providing insights into real-world implementations and outcomes. This knowledge will empower you to apply these principles effectively in your own serverless projects.

4o mini

You said:

write in 7000 words Chapter 12

ChatGPT said:

ChatGPT

Chapter 12: Case Studies in Serverless Computing

In the rapidly evolving landscape of software development, serverless computing has emerged as a transformative paradigm. Many organizations are leveraging serverless architectures to enhance scalability, reduce operational overhead, and accelerate innovation. This chapter explores various case studies of organizations that have successfully implemented serverless solutions, highlighting their unique challenges, implementations, and outcomes. By analyzing these real-world examples, we aim to provide practical insights into the benefits and considerations of adopting serverless computing.

1. Case Study: Coca-Cola

1.1. Overview
Coca-Cola, a global leader in the beverage industry, has embraced serverless computing to optimize its marketing campaigns and enhance customer engagement. The company sought to streamline data processing from various sources and gain real-time insights into customer preferences.

1.2. Challenges
Before implementing serverless solutions, Coca-Cola faced several challenges:

- **Data Silos**: Data was scattered across multiple platforms and systems, making it difficult to analyze and derive insights effectively.
- **Slow Response Times**: The existing infrastructure struggled to provide timely insights, hindering marketing teams from making data-driven decisions.
- **Resource Management**: Managing infrastructure for data processing and analytics was resource-intensive and costly.

1.3. Implementation
Coca-Cola turned to AWS serverless technologies to address these challenges:

- **AWS Lambda for Data Processing**: The company utilized AWS Lambda to process large volumes of data from various sources, including social media, sales data, and customer feedback. Lambda functions were triggered by events such as data uploads and changes, allowing for real-time processing.
- **Amazon Kinesis for Streaming Data**: Coca-Cola implemented Amazon Kinesis to collect and process streaming data in real time. This enabled the company to analyze customer interactions and respond quickly to trends.
- **Data Lake Architecture**: The organization adopted a data lake architec-

ture using Amazon S3 to store structured and unstructured data. This approach allowed for easy access to data for analysis and reporting.

1.4. Results

Coca-Cola's transition to a serverless architecture yielded significant results:

- **Enhanced Insights**: The company gained the ability to analyze customer preferences in real time, allowing marketing teams to tailor campaigns effectively.
- **Cost Reduction**: By leveraging serverless technologies, Coca-Cola reduced infrastructure costs and optimized resource utilization, allowing the company to allocate resources to strategic initiatives.
- **Faster Decision-Making**: The ability to process data quickly empowered marketing teams to make informed decisions based on real-time insights.

2. Case Study: Nordstrom

2.1. Overview

Nordstrom, a leading fashion retailer, adopted serverless computing to enhance its e-commerce platform and improve customer experience. The company sought to leverage serverless technologies to provide personalized shopping experiences and streamline its backend processes.

2.2. Challenges

Nordstrom faced several challenges that prompted its shift to serverless:

- **Scalability Issues**: The existing infrastructure struggled to handle spikes in traffic during peak shopping seasons, leading to slow website performance.
- **Personalization**: The company wanted to improve its ability to deliver personalized product recommendations based on user behavior.
- **Development Speed**: The development and deployment of new features

were slowed by the need to manage infrastructure.

2.3. Implementation

Nordstrom implemented a serverless architecture using AWS services to address these challenges:

- **AWS Lambda for Personalization**: Nordstrom used AWS Lambda to run algorithms that generate personalized product recommendations for customers. Lambda functions were triggered by user interactions, allowing for real-time recommendations.
- **Amazon DynamoDB for Data Storage**: The company utilized DynamoDB to store customer preferences and browsing history. This NoSQL database provided low-latency access to data, enhancing the user experience.
- **API Gateway for Microservices**: Nordstrom implemented API Gateway to manage its backend services, providing a scalable and secure entry point for API requests.

2.4. Results

The adoption of serverless computing led to significant improvements for Nordstrom:

- **Improved Scalability**: The serverless architecture allowed Nordstrom to handle traffic spikes seamlessly during peak shopping seasons without performance degradation.
- **Enhanced Personalization**: The ability to provide real-time product recommendations improved customer engagement and conversion rates.
- **Faster Development Cycles**: The company was able to accelerate the development and deployment of new features, allowing it to respond quickly to market demands.

3. Case Study: Netflix

3.1. Overview

Netflix, a global leader in streaming entertainment, has leveraged serverless computing to optimize its content delivery and improve user experiences. The company sought to enhance its data processing capabilities while maintaining the agility needed to innovate quickly.

3.2. Challenges

Netflix faced several challenges that drove its transition to serverless:

- **Data Processing Bottlenecks**: The existing infrastructure struggled to keep up with the massive volumes of data generated by user interactions, leading to delays in data processing.
- **Complex Architectures**: The complexity of managing numerous microservices made it challenging to maintain operational efficiency.
- **Cost Management**: The company needed to optimize costs associated with infrastructure management while ensuring high availability.

3.3. Implementation

Netflix implemented serverless technologies to address these challenges:

- **AWS Lambda for Data Processing**: The company used AWS Lambda to process user interaction data in real time. Lambda functions were triggered by events such as video plays and user ratings, allowing for immediate analysis.
- **Amazon S3 for Storage**: Netflix utilized Amazon S3 to store large volumes of content and metadata, enabling efficient access and retrieval.
- **Microservices Architecture**: The organization adopted a microservices architecture with serverless functions managing specific tasks, reducing the complexity of managing services.

3.4. Results

Netflix's transition to serverless computing yielded impressive results:

- **Real-Time Analytics**: The ability to process user interaction data in real time enhanced Netflix's recommendations and content delivery.
- **Cost Efficiency**: By leveraging serverless technologies, Netflix reduced infrastructure costs while maintaining high availability and performance.
- **Accelerated Innovation**: The company was able to innovate rapidly, deploying new features and improvements with minimal operational overhead.

4. Case Study: Expedia

4.1. Overview

Expedia, a leading online travel agency, adopted serverless computing to enhance its booking processes and improve customer experiences. The company sought to leverage serverless technologies to provide real-time availability and dynamic pricing for travel bookings.

4.2. Challenges

Expedia faced several challenges that led to its transition to serverless:

- **Performance Issues**: The existing infrastructure struggled to handle high traffic volumes during peak travel seasons, leading to slow response times.
- **Dynamic Pricing**: The company needed to implement dynamic pricing strategies based on market demand and availability.
- **Complex Architecture**: Managing a complex architecture of microservices made it challenging to scale and maintain.

4.3. Implementation

Expedia implemented a serverless architecture using AWS services to address these challenges:

- **AWS Lambda for Dynamic Pricing**: Expedia utilized AWS Lambda to implement dynamic pricing algorithms that adjust rates based on real-time demand. Lambda functions processed data from multiple sources to calculate prices.

- **Amazon API Gateway**: The company used API Gateway to manage its booking APIs, allowing seamless integration with backend services while ensuring scalability and security.
- **Amazon DynamoDB for Data Storage**: Expedia leveraged DynamoDB to store inventory and pricing information, providing fast access to data during booking processes.

4.4. Results

Expedia's adoption of serverless computing led to significant improvements:

- **Improved Scalability**: The serverless architecture allowed Expedia to handle peak travel demands without performance degradation.
- **Enhanced User Experience**: Dynamic pricing capabilities improved the accuracy of pricing information, leading to increased customer satisfaction.
- **Faster Development Cycles**: The company was able to accelerate the development and deployment of new features, improving its competitive edge in the travel industry.

5. Case Study: Samsung

5.1. Overview

Samsung, a global leader in technology and consumer electronics, leveraged serverless computing to enhance its IoT solutions and streamline data processing. The company sought to optimize its IoT platform while providing real-time insights into device performance and usage.

5.2. Challenges

Before adopting serverless technologies, Samsung faced several challenges:

- **Scalability Issues**: The existing infrastructure struggled to scale efficiently as the number of connected devices increased.

- **Data Processing Bottlenecks**: Analyzing data from numerous devices in real time posed significant challenges, hindering the ability to provide timely insights.
- **Operational Complexity**: Managing a complex architecture with multiple microservices created operational overhead.

5.3. Implementation

Samsung implemented serverless technologies to address these challenges:

- **AWS IoT Core**: Samsung utilized AWS IoT Core to manage and process data from connected devices. This service enabled seamless communication between devices and AWS services.
- **AWS Lambda for Data Processing**: The company used AWS Lambda to process incoming device data in real time, allowing for immediate analysis and reporting.
- **Amazon Kinesis for Streaming Data**: Samsung leveraged Amazon Kinesis to collect and process streaming data from its IoT devices, providing insights into device performance and usage patterns.

5.4. Results

Samsung's transition to serverless computing led to significant improvements:

- **Scalable Infrastructure**: The serverless architecture enabled Samsung to scale its IoT platform efficiently, accommodating millions of connected devices without performance issues.
- **Real-Time Insights**: The ability to process device data in real time provided Samsung with valuable insights into device performance and usage, improving customer satisfaction.
- **Reduced Operational Overhead**: By leveraging serverless technologies, Samsung minimized the complexity of managing infrastructure, allowing the company to focus on innovation.

6. Case Study: Adobe

6.1. Overview

Adobe, a leader in digital media and marketing solutions, adopted serverless computing to enhance its Creative Cloud services and streamline content processing. The company sought to leverage serverless technologies to provide a more efficient and responsive user experience.

6.2. Challenges

Adobe faced several challenges that prompted its transition to serverless:

- **Performance Bottlenecks**: The existing infrastructure struggled to deliver timely processing of large media files, impacting user experience.
- **Scalability Issues**: Handling spikes in user activity during peak times posed challenges for resource allocation and performance.
- **Operational Complexity**: Managing a complex architecture of microservices increased operational overhead.

6.3. Implementation

Adobe implemented serverless solutions using AWS services to address these challenges:

- **AWS Lambda for Media Processing**: Adobe utilized AWS Lambda to process media files uploaded by users. Functions were triggered by events such as file uploads to S3, allowing for real-time processing and transformations.
- **Amazon S3 for Storage**: Adobe leveraged Amazon S3 to store user-generated content, providing a scalable and durable storage solution.
- **API Gateway for Service Integration**: Adobe used API Gateway to manage its backend services, ensuring secure and scalable access to APIs.

6.4. Results

The adoption of serverless computing led to significant improvements for Adobe:

- **Enhanced Performance**: The ability to process media files in real time improved the overall user experience, allowing for faster uploads and transformations.
- **Scalable Architecture**: The serverless architecture enabled Adobe to handle spikes in user activity seamlessly, ensuring consistent performance during peak times.
- **Reduced Complexity**: By leveraging serverless technologies, Adobe minimized operational overhead and improved resource management.

7. Case Study: Airbnb

7.1. Overview

Airbnb, a global leader in the hospitality industry, adopted serverless computing to enhance its booking platform and improve customer experience. The company sought to leverage serverless technologies to provide real-time availability and dynamic pricing for accommodations.

7.2. Challenges

Airbnb faced several challenges that led to its transition to serverless:

- **Performance Issues**: The existing infrastructure struggled to handle high traffic volumes during peak booking periods, leading to slow response times.
- **Dynamic Pricing**: The company needed to implement dynamic pricing strategies based on market demand and availability.
- **Operational Complexity**: Managing a complex architecture with multiple microservices made it challenging to scale and maintain.

7.3. Implementation

Airbnb implemented a serverless architecture using AWS services to address these challenges:

- **AWS Lambda for Dynamic Pricing**: Airbnb utilized AWS Lambda to implement dynamic pricing algorithms that adjust rates based on real-time demand. Lambda functions processed data from multiple sources to calculate prices.

- **Amazon API Gateway**: The company used API Gateway to manage its booking APIs, allowing seamless integration with backend services while ensuring scalability and security.
- **Amazon DynamoDB for Data Storage**: Airbnb leveraged DynamoDB to store inventory and pricing information, providing fast access to data during booking processes.

7.4. Results

Airbnb's adoption of serverless computing led to significant improvements:

- **Improved Scalability**: The serverless architecture allowed Airbnb to handle peak travel demands without performance degradation.
- **Enhanced User Experience**: Dynamic pricing capabilities improved the accuracy of pricing information, leading to increased customer satisfaction.
- **Faster Development Cycles**: The company was able to accelerate the development and deployment of new features, improving its competitive edge in the hospitality industry.

8. Conclusion

In this chapter, we explored a range of case studies that highlight the successful adoption of serverless computing across various industries. Organizations like Coca-Cola, Nordstrom, Netflix, Expedia, Samsung, Adobe, and Airbnb have leveraged serverless technologies to overcome challenges, enhance performance, and improve customer experiences.

These case studies illustrate the versatility and scalability of serverless architectures, demonstrating their potential to drive innovation and efficiency in modern application development. By analyzing these real-world implementations, developers and organizations can gain valuable insights into the benefits and considerations of adopting serverless computing.

As you continue your journey into serverless architecture, consider the lessons learned from these case studies and how they can be applied to your own projects. In the next chapter, we will summarize the key takeaways from this book and provide guidance on how to implement serverless solutions effectively in your organization.

Chapter 13: Key Takeaways and Implementing Serverless Solutions

As we conclude our exploration of serverless computing, it's essential to reflect on the key takeaways from this journey and provide practical guidance on implementing serverless solutions effectively in your organization. This chapter will summarize the fundamental concepts covered in previous chapters, discuss the best practices for transitioning to serverless architectures, and offer a roadmap for successfully implementing serverless solutions. By understanding these key aspects, organizations can leverage the power of serverless computing to enhance their applications and drive innovation.

1. Recap of Serverless Computing Concepts

1.1. What is Serverless Computing?

Serverless computing is a cloud computing paradigm that allows developers to build and run applications without managing server infrastructure. Instead, cloud providers automatically handle server management, scaling, and resource allocation, enabling developers to focus on writing code.

1.2. Benefits of Serverless Architecture

Serverless architectures offer numerous advantages, including:

- **Reduced Operational Overhead**: Developers can deploy applications without worrying about server management, reducing the operational burden on IT teams.
- **Automatic Scaling**: Serverless platforms automatically scale resources based on demand, allowing applications to handle varying loads without manual intervention.
- **Cost Efficiency**: Organizations pay only for the compute resources used during function execution, which can lead to significant cost savings compared to traditional hosting models.
- **Faster Time to Market**: With serverless computing, developers can quickly build and deploy applications, accelerating the delivery of new features and services.

1.3. Key Components of Serverless Architectures

Serverless architectures consist of several key components:

- **Serverless Functions**: These are the core units of serverless applications, typically deployed as small, stateless functions that respond to events.
- **Event Sources**: Events can originate from various sources, such as user actions, database changes, or external services, triggering the execution of serverless functions.
- **APIs**: Serverless applications often expose APIs through services like API Gateway, enabling communication between frontend applications and backend services.
- **Data Storage**: Serverless applications rely on various data storage solutions, such as NoSQL databases (e.g., DynamoDB), relational databases (e.g., RDS), and object storage (e.g., S3).

2. Best Practices for Implementing Serverless Solutions

As organizations consider transitioning to serverless architectures, several best practices should guide the implementation process:

2.1. Start with Clear Objectives

Before adopting serverless computing, organizations should define clear objectives for their serverless applications. Consider the following questions:

- What problems are you trying to solve with serverless computing?
- How will serverless architectures align with your overall business goals?
- What key performance indicators (KPIs) will you use to measure success?

By establishing clear objectives, organizations can ensure that their serverless initiatives are aligned with their strategic goals.

2.2. Assess Current Workloads

Evaluate existing workloads to determine which applications are suitable for migration to serverless architectures. Consider factors such as:

- **Frequency of Usage**: Workloads with unpredictable usage patterns may benefit most from serverless architectures.
- **Scalability Requirements**: Applications requiring rapid scaling during peak loads are excellent candidates for serverless.
- **Statelessness**: Serverless functions are stateless, so applications that can be designed as stateless services are more suitable for this architecture.

2.3. Choose the Right Tools and Frameworks

Selecting the right tools and frameworks is essential for a successful serverless implementation. Consider the following:

- **Cloud Provider**: Evaluate the offerings of different cloud providers (e.g., AWS, Azure, Google Cloud) and choose one that aligns with your organization's needs and expertise.
- **Serverless Frameworks**: Leverage serverless frameworks like the Serverless Framework, AWS SAM, or AWS Chalice to streamline development and deployment processes.
- **Monitoring and Observability Tools**: Implement monitoring tools such as AWS CloudWatch, Azure Monitor, or third-party solutions to track application performance and detect issues.

2.4. Implement Security Best Practices

Security is a critical aspect of serverless computing. Follow these best practices to secure your serverless applications:

- **Use IAM Roles and Policies**: Implement the principle of least privilege by assigning appropriate IAM roles and policies to serverless functions.
- **Secure APIs**: Protect APIs with authentication and authorization mechanisms, such as AWS Cognito or OAuth2.
- **Encrypt Sensitive Data**: Ensure that sensitive data is encrypted both in transit and at rest using services like AWS KMS.

2.5. Embrace Continuous Integration and Deployment

Implementing CI/CD practices is essential for efficiently managing serverless applications:

- **Automated Testing**: Integrate automated testing into your CI/CD pipeline to catch bugs early in the development process.
- **Canary and Blue/Green Deployments**: Use deployment strategies like canary or blue/green deployments to minimize risks during updates.
- **Version Control**: Maintain version control for both application code and infrastructure as code (IaC) configurations.

3. Roadmap for Transitioning to Serverless Architectures

Transitioning to serverless architectures requires careful planning and execution. The following roadmap outlines the key steps for successfully implementing serverless solutions:

3.1. Define Your Strategy

- **Identify Use Cases**: Determine which applications or services are suitable for migration to serverless architectures.
- **Set Goals and KPIs**: Establish clear goals for your serverless initiatives and define KPIs to measure success.

3.2. Conduct a Proof of Concept (PoC)

- **Select a Small Project**: Start with a small project or application to experiment with serverless technologies and validate their feasibility.
- **Evaluate Performance**: Monitor the performance of the PoC and gather feedback from stakeholders to identify areas for improvement.

3.3. Build the Core Team

- **Assemble a Cross-Functional Team**: Build a team that includes developers, operations, security, and business stakeholders to ensure a holistic approach to serverless implementation.
- **Provide Training**: Offer training and resources to team members to build expertise in serverless technologies and best practices.

3.4. Design and Develop Serverless Solutions

- **Architect for Scalability**: Design serverless applications with scalability in mind, using event-driven architectures and microservices principles.
- **Leverage Serverless Frameworks**: Use serverless frameworks to streamline development and deployment processes.

3.5. Implement Security and Compliance Measures

- **Define Security Policies**: Establish security policies and practices to protect serverless applications from potential threats.
- **Conduct Compliance Audits**: Ensure that serverless applications comply with relevant regulations and industry standards.

3.6. Monitor and Optimize

- **Implement Monitoring Tools**: Use monitoring and observability tools to track application performance and detect issues in real time.

- **Continuous Optimization**: Regularly assess and optimize serverless applications based on performance data and user feedback.

4. Real-World Challenges and Solutions

While serverless computing offers numerous advantages, organizations may encounter challenges during implementation. Here are common challenges and potential solutions:

4.1. Cold Start Latency

Challenge: Cold starts can introduce latency in serverless applications, impacting user experience.

Solution: Implement provisioned concurrency for critical functions to keep them warm and reduce cold start times. Additionally, optimize the size of deployment packages to minimize loading times.

4.2. Vendor Lock-In

Challenge: Organizations may worry about vendor lock-in when adopting specific cloud providers' serverless solutions.

Solution: Design applications using open standards and frameworks to facilitate easier migration between cloud providers. Consider multi-cloud strategies to mitigate vendor lock-in risks.

4.3. Debugging Complexity

Challenge: Debugging serverless applications can be challenging due to their distributed nature and statelessness.

Solution: Implement structured logging and distributed tracing to gain insights into application behavior. Utilize tools like AWS X-Ray to visualize request flows and identify bottlenecks.

5. The Future of Serverless Computing

5.1. Continuous Evolution

The serverless computing landscape is continually evolving, with new features and services being introduced regularly. Organizations should stay informed about emerging technologies and trends to remain competitive.

5.2. Community and Ecosystem Growth

As serverless computing gains traction, the developer community and ecosystem will expand. Organizations can benefit from increased collaboration, knowledge sharing, and the availability of resources.

5.3. Integration with Emerging Technologies

The integration of serverless computing with emerging technologies such as AI, machine learning, and edge computing will unlock new possibilities for application development and deployment.

6. Conclusion

In this chapter, we explored the key takeaways from our journey into serverless computing and provided practical guidance for implementing serverless solutions effectively. By understanding the fundamental concepts, following best practices, and addressing common challenges, organizations can leverage the power of serverless computing to enhance their applications and drive innovation.

As you embark on your serverless journey, keep in mind that successful implementation requires careful planning, ongoing monitoring, and a willingness to adapt to changing technologies and practices. With the right approach, serverless computing can unlock new opportunities for growth and transformation in your organization.

4o mini

You said:

write in 7000 words Chapter 14

ChatGPT said:

ChatGPT

Chapter 14: Transitioning to Serverless Architecture: A Step-by-Step Guide

Transitioning to serverless architecture can seem daunting, especially for organizations entrenched in traditional computing models. However, with a structured approach and clear guidance, this transition can lead to significant benefits, including increased scalability, reduced operational overhead, and enhanced innovation. This chapter provides a comprehensive, step-by-step guide for organizations looking to migrate to serverless architecture. We will cover the entire transition process, from initial planning to execution and ongoing management.

1. Understanding the Transition to Serverless Architecture

1.1. What is Serverless Architecture?

Serverless architecture is a cloud computing model where the cloud provider dynamically manages the allocation of machine resources. Developers can build and run applications without managing the underlying infrastructure. Instead of provisioning servers, developers deploy functions or applications that execute in response to events, and the cloud provider handles scaling, availability, and fault tolerance.

1.2. Benefits of Serverless Architecture

Before embarking on the transition, it's essential to understand the benefits serverless architecture offers:

- **Cost Efficiency**: Organizations pay only for the compute resources used during function execution, which can significantly reduce operational costs.
- **Scalability**: Serverless architectures automatically scale based on demand, allowing applications to handle traffic spikes seamlessly without manual intervention.
- **Faster Time to Market**: Developers can focus on writing code and deploying applications quickly, accelerating the delivery of new features

and services.

- **Reduced Operational Overhead**: With serverless computing, organizations can offload infrastructure management tasks to cloud providers, freeing up IT teams to focus on strategic initiatives.

2. Preparing for the Transition

2.1. Assess Current Infrastructure and Workloads

The first step in transitioning to serverless architecture is assessing the current infrastructure and workloads. This assessment should include:

- **Inventory Existing Applications**: Identify all applications and services currently running on traditional infrastructure.
- **Evaluate Workload Characteristics**: Determine the usage patterns, traffic variability, and scaling requirements of each application. Workloads that are event-driven or have unpredictable usage patterns are often the best candidates for serverless migration.
- **Identify Dependencies**: Analyze dependencies between applications, databases, and third-party services to understand the impact of migration on existing systems.

2.2. Define Objectives and Goals

Setting clear objectives and goals for the transition is crucial to ensuring a successful migration. Consider the following:

- **Business Objectives**: Identify how adopting serverless architecture aligns with broader business goals, such as improving customer experiences, increasing efficiency, or reducing costs.
- **Key Performance Indicators (KPIs)**: Establish KPIs to measure the success of the transition, such as application performance, cost savings, and time to market for new features.

2.3. Build a Cross-Functional Team

Assemble a cross-functional team to oversee the transition process. This team should include:

- **Developers**: Responsible for writing and deploying serverless functions and applications.
- **Operations Teams**: Focused on infrastructure management, monitoring, and security.
- **Business Stakeholders**: Provide input on business objectives and ensure alignment with organizational goals.
- **Security Experts**: Ensure that security considerations are integrated into the transition process from the beginning.

3. Developing a Migration Strategy

3.1. Choose the Right Cloud Provider

Selecting the right cloud provider is a critical decision in the transition to serverless architecture. Consider the following factors:

- **Service Offerings**: Evaluate the serverless services provided by each cloud provider, such as AWS Lambda, Azure Functions, and Google Cloud Functions.
- **Integration Capabilities**: Consider how well the cloud provider's services integrate with existing applications and services.
- **Cost Structure**: Analyze the pricing models of different providers to understand potential costs based on expected usage.

3.2. Create a Roadmap for Migration

Develop a detailed roadmap that outlines the steps for transitioning to serverless architecture. This roadmap should include:

- **Timeline**: Establish a timeline for the migration process, including key milestones and deadlines.
- **Phases of Migration**: Break the migration process into manageable

phases, such as:

- **Phase 1: Proof of Concept (PoC)**: Start with a small project or application to test the serverless model and validate its feasibility.
- **Phase 2: Application Refactoring**: Refactor existing applications to take advantage of serverless capabilities.
- **Phase 3: Full Migration**: Gradually migrate additional applications and services based on lessons learned from earlier phases.

3.3. Develop a Change Management Plan

Implementing serverless architecture may require changes in workflows, processes, and team dynamics. Develop a change management plan that includes:

- **Stakeholder Communication**: Keep stakeholders informed about the transition process, potential impacts, and benefits.
- **Training and Resources**: Provide training and resources to help team members adapt to new technologies and practices.
- **Feedback Mechanisms**: Establish channels for team members to provide feedback and raise concerns during the transition.

4. Executing the Migration

4.1. Conducting a Proof of Concept (PoC)

Before migrating entire applications, it's advisable to conduct a proof of concept (PoC) to validate serverless architecture for your organization. This involves:

- **Selecting a Use Case**: Choose a small application or component with limited complexity for the PoC.
- **Building a Serverless Prototype**: Develop a prototype using serverless technologies, following best practices for architecture and design.
- **Measuring Performance**: Evaluate the performance, scalability, and cost of the serverless prototype against established KPIs.

4.2. Refactoring Applications for Serverless

Once the PoC is validated, begin refactoring existing applications for serverless architecture:

- **Identify Stateless Components**: Break down applications into stateless components that can be implemented as serverless functions.
- **Implement Event-Driven Patterns**: Redesign applications to respond to events generated by user actions, system changes, or external services.
- **Utilize Serverless Data Stores**: Replace traditional databases with serverless data stores like Amazon DynamoDB or Azure Cosmos DB, ensuring low-latency access to data.

4.3. Gradual Migration of Services

Implement a gradual migration strategy to transition services to serverless architecture:

- **Service-by-Service Migration**: Migrate individual services or components rather than attempting a complete overhaul. This allows for incremental testing and validation.
- **Monitor and Optimize**: Continuously monitor the performance of migrated services and optimize configurations as necessary.
- **Establish Rollback Procedures**: Implement rollback procedures to revert to the previous architecture if issues arise during migration.

5. Post-Migration Management and Optimization

5.1. Monitor Performance and Costs

After completing the migration, it's essential to monitor the performance and costs of serverless applications:

- **Implement Monitoring Tools**: Use monitoring tools like AWS Cloud-Watch or Azure Monitor to track performance metrics, invocation counts, and execution durations.

145

- **Analyze Cost Data**: Regularly analyze cost data to identify trends and optimize resource usage.

5.2. Optimize Application Performance

Continue to optimize the performance of serverless applications after migration:

- **Performance Tuning**: Fine-tune configurations, such as memory allocation and timeout settings, to improve performance based on observed usage patterns.
- **Caching Strategies**: Implement caching strategies to reduce latency and improve response times for frequently accessed data.
- **Review Function Code**: Periodically review and optimize function code to ensure it remains efficient and maintainable.

5.3. Conduct Regular Security Audits

Security remains a critical concern in serverless architectures. Conduct regular security audits to identify vulnerabilities and ensure compliance:

- **Review IAM Policies**: Regularly review IAM roles and policies to ensure they follow the principle of least privilege.
- **Monitor Logs for Anomalies**: Use centralized logging and monitoring to detect unusual activity or potential security incidents.
- **Stay Informed about Security Best Practices**: Continuously update your knowledge of security best practices and emerging threats in the serverless landscape.

6. Real-World Challenges and How to Overcome Them

While transitioning to serverless architecture offers numerous benefits, organizations may encounter challenges along the way. Here are some common challenges and strategies to address them:

6.1. Complexity of Distributed Systems

Challenge: Serverless applications often consist of multiple microservices and functions, leading to increased complexity in managing distributed systems.

Solution: Use centralized monitoring and logging solutions to gain visibility into application behavior. Implement distributed tracing to track requests as they move through different services, helping identify bottlenecks and performance issues.

6.2. Cold Start Latency

Challenge: Cold starts can introduce latency in serverless applications, especially for infrequently used functions.

Solution: Utilize provisioned concurrency for critical functions that require low latency. Additionally, optimize the deployment package size to minimize cold start times.

6.3. Managing Dependencies

Challenge: Managing dependencies between different serverless functions and services can be challenging.

Solution: Use versioning for dependencies to ensure compatibility across functions. Implement automated testing to catch issues related to dependencies before deployment.

7. The Future of Serverless Architecture

As serverless computing continues to evolve, several trends and advancements are shaping its future:

7.1. Increased Adoption of Multi-Cloud Strategies

Organizations are increasingly adopting multi-cloud strategies to avoid vendor lock-in and enhance resilience. Serverless computing fits well into this trend, allowing organizations to leverage the best services from multiple cloud providers.

7.2. Enhanced Security Measures

As the serverless landscape matures, security will remain a top priority. Cloud providers will continue to develop advanced security features and tools to protect serverless applications from emerging threats.

7.3. Integration with AI and Machine Learning

The integration of AI and machine learning with serverless architectures will unlock new possibilities for application development. Organizations will leverage serverless technologies to build intelligent applications that can analyze data and make predictions in real time.

8. Conclusion

Transitioning to serverless architecture presents a significant opportunity for organizations to enhance their applications and drive innovation. By understanding the key concepts of serverless computing, following best practices for implementation, and addressing common challenges, organizations can successfully navigate the transition and unlock the full potential of serverless architecture.

As you embark on this journey, remember to remain adaptable and open to new technologies and practices. The serverless landscape is continually evolving, and organizations that embrace change will be best positioned to thrive in the future. By implementing serverless solutions effectively, your organization can achieve greater scalability, reduced operational overhead, and improved customer experiences, ultimately driving success in today's fast-paced digital world.

Chapter 14: Implementing Serverless Solutions: A Practical Guide

As organizations move towards serverless computing, the implementation of serverless solutions requires careful planning, execution, and ongoing management. This chapter provides a practical guide to implementing serverless solutions effectively, covering each step of the process in detail. By following this guide, organizations can leverage serverless architecture to improve scalability, reduce operational costs, and enhance overall application performance.

1. Preparing for Implementation

1.1. Assessing Current Infrastructure

Before implementing serverless solutions, it is crucial to assess your current infrastructure. This assessment will help identify which applications and services are suitable for migration to a serverless model.

- **Inventory Existing Applications**: Create a comprehensive list of all applications and services currently in use, along with their architecture, usage patterns, and resource requirements.
- **Analyze Workload Characteristics**: Evaluate the workloads of each application. Identify workloads that are event-driven, have unpredictable

usage patterns, or require high scalability.

- **Identify Dependencies**: Document any dependencies between applications, databases, and third-party services to understand how migration might impact existing systems.

1.2. Defining Objectives and Goals

Establishing clear objectives and goals is essential for a successful serverless implementation. Consider the following:

- **Business Objectives**: Align serverless initiatives with broader business goals. Determine how serverless computing can help improve customer experiences, increase efficiency, or reduce costs.
- **Key Performance Indicators (KPIs)**: Define KPIs to measure the success of your serverless solutions. These may include application performance metrics, cost savings, and time-to-market for new features.

1.3. Building a Cross-Functional Team

Creating a cross-functional team is critical for overseeing the implementation of serverless solutions. This team should include:

- **Developers**: Responsible for writing and deploying serverless functions and applications.
- **Operations Teams**: Focused on infrastructure management, monitoring, and security.
- **Business Stakeholders**: Provide input on business objectives and ensure alignment with organizational goals.
- **Security Experts**: Ensure that security considerations are integrated into the implementation process from the outset.

2. Developing a Migration Strategy

2.1. Choosing the Right Cloud Provider

Selecting the right cloud provider is a critical decision in the transition to serverless architecture. Consider the following factors:

- **Service Offerings**: Evaluate the serverless services provided by each cloud provider, such as AWS Lambda, Azure Functions, and Google Cloud Functions.
- **Integration Capabilities**: Consider how well the cloud provider's services integrate with existing applications and services.
- **Cost Structure**: Analyze the pricing models of different providers to understand potential costs based on expected usage.

2.2. Creating a Roadmap for Migration

Develop a detailed roadmap that outlines the steps for transitioning to serverless architecture. This roadmap should include:

- **Timeline**: Establish a timeline for the migration process, including key milestones and deadlines.
- **Phases of Migration**: Break the migration process into manageable phases, such as:
- **Phase 1: Proof of Concept (PoC)**: Start with a small project or application to test the serverless model and validate its feasibility.
- **Phase 2: Application Refactoring**: Refactor existing applications to take advantage of serverless capabilities.
- **Phase 3: Full Migration**: Gradually migrate additional applications and services based on lessons learned from earlier phases.

2.3. Developing a Change Management Plan

Implementing serverless architecture may require changes in workflows, processes, and team dynamics. Develop a change management plan that includes:

151

- **Stakeholder Communication**: Keep stakeholders informed about the transition process, potential impacts, and benefits.
- **Training and Resources**: Provide training and resources to help team members adapt to new technologies and practices.
- **Feedback Mechanisms**: Establish channels for team members to provide feedback and raise concerns during the transition.

3. Executing the Migration

3.1. Conducting a Proof of Concept (PoC)

Before migrating entire applications, it's advisable to conduct a proof of concept (PoC) to validate serverless architecture for your organization. This involves:

- **Selecting a Use Case**: Choose a small application or component with limited complexity for the PoC.
- **Building a Serverless Prototype**: Develop a prototype using serverless technologies, following best practices for architecture and design.
- **Measuring Performance**: Evaluate the performance, scalability, and cost of the serverless prototype against established KPIs.

3.2. Refactoring Applications for Serverless

Once the PoC is validated, begin refactoring existing applications for serverless architecture:

- **Identify Stateless Components**: Break down applications into stateless components that can be implemented as serverless functions.
- **Implement Event-Driven Patterns**: Redesign applications to respond to events generated by user actions, system changes, or external services.
- **Utilize Serverless Data Stores**: Replace traditional databases with serverless data stores like Amazon DynamoDB or Azure Cosmos DB, ensuring low-latency access to data.

3.3. Gradual Migration of Services

Implement a gradual migration strategy to transition services to serverless architecture:

- **Service-by-Service Migration**: Migrate individual services or components rather than attempting a complete overhaul. This allows for incremental testing and validation.
- **Monitor and Optimize**: Continuously monitor the performance of migrated services and optimize configurations as necessary.
- **Establish Rollback Procedures**: Implement rollback procedures to revert to the previous architecture if issues arise during migration.

4. Post-Migration Management and Optimization

4.1. Monitor Performance and Costs

After completing the migration, it's essential to monitor the performance and costs of serverless applications:

- **Implement Monitoring Tools**: Use monitoring tools like AWS CloudWatch or Azure Monitor to track performance metrics, invocation counts, and execution durations.
- **Analyze Cost Data**: Regularly analyze cost data to identify trends and optimize resource usage.

4.2. Optimize Application Performance

Continue to optimize the performance of serverless applications after migration:

- **Performance Tuning**: Fine-tune configurations, such as memory allocation and timeout settings, to improve performance based on observed usage patterns.
- **Caching Strategies**: Implement caching strategies to reduce latency and improve response times for frequently accessed data.

- **Review Function Code**: Periodically review and optimize function code to ensure it remains efficient and maintainable.

4.3. Conduct Regular Security Audits

Security remains a critical concern in serverless architectures. Conduct regular security audits to identify vulnerabilities and ensure compliance:

- **Review IAM Policies**: Regularly review IAM roles and policies to ensure they follow the principle of least privilege.
- **Monitor Logs for Anomalies**: Use centralized logging and monitoring to detect unusual activity or potential security incidents.
- **Stay Informed about Security Best Practices**: Continuously update your knowledge of security best practices and emerging threats in the serverless landscape.

5. Real-World Challenges and Solutions

While transitioning to serverless architecture offers numerous benefits, organizations may encounter challenges during implementation. Here are common challenges and potential solutions:

5.1. Complexity of Distributed Systems

Challenge: Serverless applications often consist of multiple microservices and functions, leading to increased complexity in managing distributed systems.

Solution: Use centralized monitoring and logging solutions to gain visibility into application behavior. Implement distributed tracing to track requests as they move through different services, helping identify bottlenecks and performance issues.

5.2. Cold Start Latency

Challenge: Cold starts can introduce latency in serverless applications, especially for infrequently used functions.

Solution: Utilize provisioned concurrency for critical functions that require low latency. Additionally, optimize the deployment package size to minimize cold start times.

5.3. Managing Dependencies

Challenge: Managing dependencies between different serverless functions and services can be challenging.

Solution: Use versioning for dependencies to ensure compatibility across functions. Implement automated testing to catch issues related to dependencies before deployment.

6. The Future of Serverless Architecture

6.1. Continuous Evolution

The serverless computing landscape is continually evolving, with new features and services being introduced regularly. Organizations should stay informed about emerging technologies and trends to remain competitive.

6.2. Community and Ecosystem Growth

As serverless computing gains traction, the developer community and ecosystem will expand. Organizations can benefit from increased collaboration, knowledge sharing, and the availability of resources.

6.3. Integration with Emerging Technologies

The integration of serverless computing with emerging technologies such as AI, machine learning, and edge computing will unlock new possibilities for application development and deployment.

7. Conclusion

Transitioning to serverless architecture presents a significant opportunity for organizations to enhance their applications and drive innovation. By understanding the key concepts of serverless computing, following best practices for implementation, and addressing common challenges, organizations can successfully navigate the transition and unlock the full potential of serverless architecture.

As you embark on this journey, remember to remain adaptable and open to new technologies and practices. The serverless landscape is continually evolving, and organizations that embrace change will be best positioned to thrive in the future. By implementing serverless solutions effectively, your organization can achieve greater scalability, reduced operational overhead, and improved customer experiences, ultimately driving success in today's fast-paced digital world.

This chapter provides a structured approach to transitioning to serverless architecture, encompassing preparation, execution, post-migration management, and an overview of real-world challenges and solutions. Following this guide will help organizations successfully implement serverless solutions and capitalize on the benefits of this innovative computing model.

Conclusion: Embracing the Future of Serverless Computing

As we reach the conclusion of this comprehensive exploration of serverless computing, it's essential to reflect on the key insights, lessons learned, and the future trajectory of this transformative technology. Serverless architecture has emerged as a game changer in the world of application development, offering organizations unprecedented flexibility, scalability, and cost efficiency. By understanding the principles, benefits, challenges, and best practices associated with serverless computing, organizations can harness its full potential to drive innovation and enhance their digital offerings.

1. Recap of Key Insights

1.1. Definition and Evolution of Serverless Computing

Serverless computing allows developers to build and run applications without the need to manage server infrastructure. Instead of provisioning and maintaining servers, developers can deploy functions that execute in response to events, with cloud providers automatically handling the scaling and management of resources. This paradigm shift has evolved from traditional cloud models, driven by the need for greater agility and responsiveness in an increasingly digital world.

1.2. Benefits of Serverless Architecture

The transition to serverless architecture offers numerous benefits that can significantly impact organizational performance:

Cost Efficiency: Organizations pay only for the compute resources they consume, leading to lower operational costs compared to traditional models where resources must be provisioned ahead of time.

Scalability: Serverless architectures automatically scale to handle fluctuating demand, allowing applications to maintain performance during peak traffic periods without manual intervention.

Faster Time to Market: The ease of deploying serverless functions enables rapid development and iteration, allowing organizations to launch new features and services more quickly.

Reduced Operational Overhead: With the cloud provider managing infrastructure, IT teams can focus on higher-level strategic initiatives rather than day-to-day operational tasks.

1.3. Key Components of Serverless Architectures

Successful serverless implementations rely on several key components, including:

Serverless Functions: These small, stateless units of code execute in response to events and are the core of serverless applications.

Event Sources: Events can trigger serverless functions from various sources, such as user actions, database changes, or external services.

APIs: Serverless applications often expose APIs through gateways, allowing communication between frontend applications and backend services.

Data Storage: Serverless architectures leverage various data storage solutions, including NoSQL databases and object storage, to support application requirements.

2. Best Practices for Successful Implementation

Throughout the book, we highlighted numerous best practices that organizations should follow when implementing serverless solutions:

2.1. Clear Objectives and Goals

Defining clear objectives and goals is crucial for guiding serverless initiatives. Organizations should align their serverless strategies with broader business goals, such as improving customer experiences, increasing operational efficiency, or reducing costs.

2.2. Thorough Assessment and Planning

A thorough assessment of existing infrastructure and workloads is essential before transitioning to serverless. By analyzing current applications and their characteristics, organizations can identify the best candidates for migration.

2.3. Choosing the Right Cloud Provider

Selecting the appropriate cloud provider is a critical decision that impacts the success of serverless implementations. Organizations should evaluate service offerings, integration capabilities, and pricing models before making their choice.

2.4. Gradual Migration Strategy

Implementing a gradual migration strategy allows organizations to test and validate serverless solutions before full-scale adoption. Starting with a proof of concept (PoC) can provide valuable insights and build confidence in the serverless model.

2.5. Continuous Monitoring and Optimization

Once serverless applications are deployed, continuous monitoring and optimization are essential. Organizations should implement monitoring tools to track performance, analyze cost data, and identify areas for improvement.

3. Real-World Applications and Success Stories

The case studies presented throughout the book showcased how leading organizations have successfully leveraged serverless computing to address their unique challenges:

Coca-Cola: By implementing serverless technologies, Coca-Cola streamlined its data processing and gained real-time insights into customer preferences, ultimately enhancing its marketing efforts.

Nordstrom: Nordstrom utilized serverless architecture to improve its e-commerce platform, providing personalized shopping experiences and increasing scalability during peak shopping seasons.

Netflix: With serverless computing, Netflix optimized its content delivery and data processing capabilities, allowing for faster innovation and improved user experiences.

Expedia: By adopting serverless solutions, Expedia enhanced its booking processes, implemented dynamic pricing strategies, and improved customer satisfaction.

These examples illustrate the versatility and effectiveness of serverless computing across various industries, demonstrating its potential to drive innovation and operational excellence.

4. Challenges and Considerations

Despite the numerous advantages of serverless computing, organizations may encounter challenges during the transition:

4.1. Complexity of Distributed Systems

Serverless applications often consist of multiple microservices and functions, leading to increased complexity in managing distributed systems. Organizations should implement centralized monitoring and logging solutions to gain visibility into application behavior and performance.

4.2. Cold Start Latency

Cold starts can introduce latency in serverless applications, particularly for infrequently used functions. Utilizing provisioned concurrency for critical functions and optimizing deployment package sizes can help mitigate cold start impacts.

4.3. Managing Dependencies

Managing dependencies between different serverless functions and services can be challenging. Organizations should use versioning for dependencies and implement automated testing to catch issues before deployment.

5. The Future of Serverless Computing

Looking ahead, several trends and advancements are poised to shape the future of serverless computing:

5.1. Increased Adoption of Multi-Cloud Strategies

Organizations are increasingly adopting multi-cloud strategies to avoid vendor lock-in and enhance resilience. Serverless computing fits well into this trend, allowing organizations to leverage the best services from multiple cloud providers.

5.2. Enhanced Security Measures

As the serverless landscape matures, security will remain a top priority. Cloud providers are continuously developing advanced security features and tools to protect serverless applications from emerging threats.

5.3. Integration with AI and Machine Learning

The integration of AI and machine learning with serverless architectures will unlock new possibilities for application development. Organizations can leverage serverless technologies to build intelligent applications capable of analyzing data and making predictions in real time.

6. Final Thoughts

In conclusion, serverless computing represents a paradigm shift in application development and deployment. By embracing serverless architecture, organizations can enhance their agility, scalability, and cost-efficiency while focusing on delivering value to their customers.

The journey to adopting serverless solutions may present challenges, but with careful planning, a commitment to best practices, and a willingness to adapt, organizations can successfully navigate this transition. The potential benefits of serverless computing are vast, and the opportunities for innovation are boundless.

As you move forward in your exploration of serverless computing, remember to remain open to new technologies and practices. The serverless landscape is continuously evolving, and organizations that embrace change will be best positioned to thrive in the future. By leveraging the insights and strategies outlined in this book, you can harness the power of serverless architecture to drive success and achieve your organizational goals in today's fast-paced digital environment.

www.ingramcontent.com/pod-product-compliance
Lightning Source LLC
LaVergne TN
LVHW022124060326
832903LV00063B/3639